Elementary Book

The aim of this book is to support the National Curriculum using the French language.

The SKOLDO™ Elementary Book is an introduction to the French language and only includes basic conversational French and vocabulary.

It is cross-curricular and designed to appeal to children of all abilities in years R, 1 and 2.

There is ample support for non-specialist teachers of French and every effort has been made to ensure that teaching and learning French with SKOLDO™ is a fun and rewarding experience.

Each lesson is divided into three parts

:1 Whole class activity based on oral listening

:2 Specifically aimed at writers

:3 Whole class activity not requiring writing

FELT SQUARES

The felt game is a firm favourite.

In order to play the game you will need to buy from a craft shop 11 felt squares.

red	yellow	blue	green	orange	
black	purple	white	grey	pink	brown

Track record for each class using Skoldo Elementary Book

	p1	p2	p4	p5	p6	p8	p9	p11	p12	p14	p15	p16	p18	p19	p21	p22	p24	p25	p26
Class:																			
Class:																			
Class:																			
Class:																			
Class:																			

	p28	p29	p31	p32	p34	p35	p36	p38	p39	p40	p41	p43	p44	p45	p47	p48	p49	p51	p52
Class:																			
Class:																			
Class:																			
Class:																			
Class:																			

Elementary Book Contents

1	**les couleurs (i)** (colours)	red yellow pink green blue
2	**les couleurs (ii)** (colours)	purple black grey orange brown
3	**song**	**Frère Jacques** (Traditional)
4	**les nombres (i)** (numbers)	1 2 3 4 5
5	**les nombres (ii)** (numbers)	6 7 8 9 10
6	**picture (i)**	Bonjour! Présent! Présente!
7	**song**	**Un oiseau, deux oiseaux** (Skoldo)
8	**game**	numbers 1 - 10
9	**les révisions**	pages 1 - 5
10	**song**	**Cinq petits vers** (Skoldo)
11	**les vêtements (i)** (clothes)	jumper jeans skirt shirt dress
12	**les vêtements (ii)** (clothes)	tee-shirt shoe trainer sock trousers
13	**song**	**Où est le grand lion?** (Skoldo)
14	**J'ai faim. (i)** (I'm hungry)	butter cheese bread milk jam
15	**J'ai faim. (ii)** (I'm hungry)	honey egg yoghurt chips pasta
16	**picture (ii)**	Comment tu t'appelles? Je m'appelle ......
17	**song**	**Savez-vous planter les choux?** (Traditional)
18	**game**	Snakes and Ladders
19	**les révisions**	pages 11 - 15
20	**song**	**Je vois deux chaussettes** (Skoldo)
21	**les animaux (i)** (animals)	cat dog fish rabbit hamster
22	**les animaux (ii)** (animals)	sheep pig cow hen horse
23	**song**	**Toc! Toc! Toc!** (Skoldo)
24	**les fruits** (fruit)	banana apple pear strawberry lemon
25	**les légumes** (vegetables)	carrot tomato onion potato cauliflower
26	**picture (iii)**	Quel âge as-tu? J'ai ....ans.
27	**song**	**J'adore les glaces.** (Skoldo)
28	**picture**	traditional children's stories
29	**les révisions**	pages 21 - 25
30	**song**	**La soupe aux légumes** (Skoldo)
31	**la tête** (head)	hair eyes mouth nose ears
32	**le corps** (body)	arm leg hand foot head
33	**song**	**Alouette** (Traditional)
34	**les passe-temps** (hobbies)	television reading swimming football cooking
35	**les jouets** (toys)	book teddy doll ball video game
36	**picture (iv)**	Où habites-tu ? J'habite à ....
37	**song**	**C'est mon anniversaire** (Skoldo)
38	**picture**	mes jeux
39	**les révisions**	pages 31 - 35
40	**la campagne (i)** (coutryside)	flower butterfly tree river bridge
41	**la campagne (ii)** (coutryside)	fox hare mouse hedgehog mole
42	**song**	**Sur le pont d'Avignon** (Traditional)
43	**la plage** (beach)	sun sea spade seagull bucket
44	**le transport** (transport)	car bike aeroplane train bus
45	**picture (v)**	Ça va? Ça va bien, merci.
46	**song**	**Un kilomètre en vélo** (Skoldo)
47	**picture**	ma famille
48	**les révisions**	pages 40 - 44
49	**chez moi** (at home)	table chair window door house
50	**la famille** (family)	mother father brother sister family
51	**song**	**Papa, Maman, David, Anne** (Skoldo)
52	**J'ai soif.** (I'm thirsty.)	water coffee tea orange juice coca cola
53	**la trousse** (pencil case)	pencil pen ruler pencil sharpener rubber
54	**song**	**Bonne nuit, dors bien** (Skoldo)

Mon nom ....

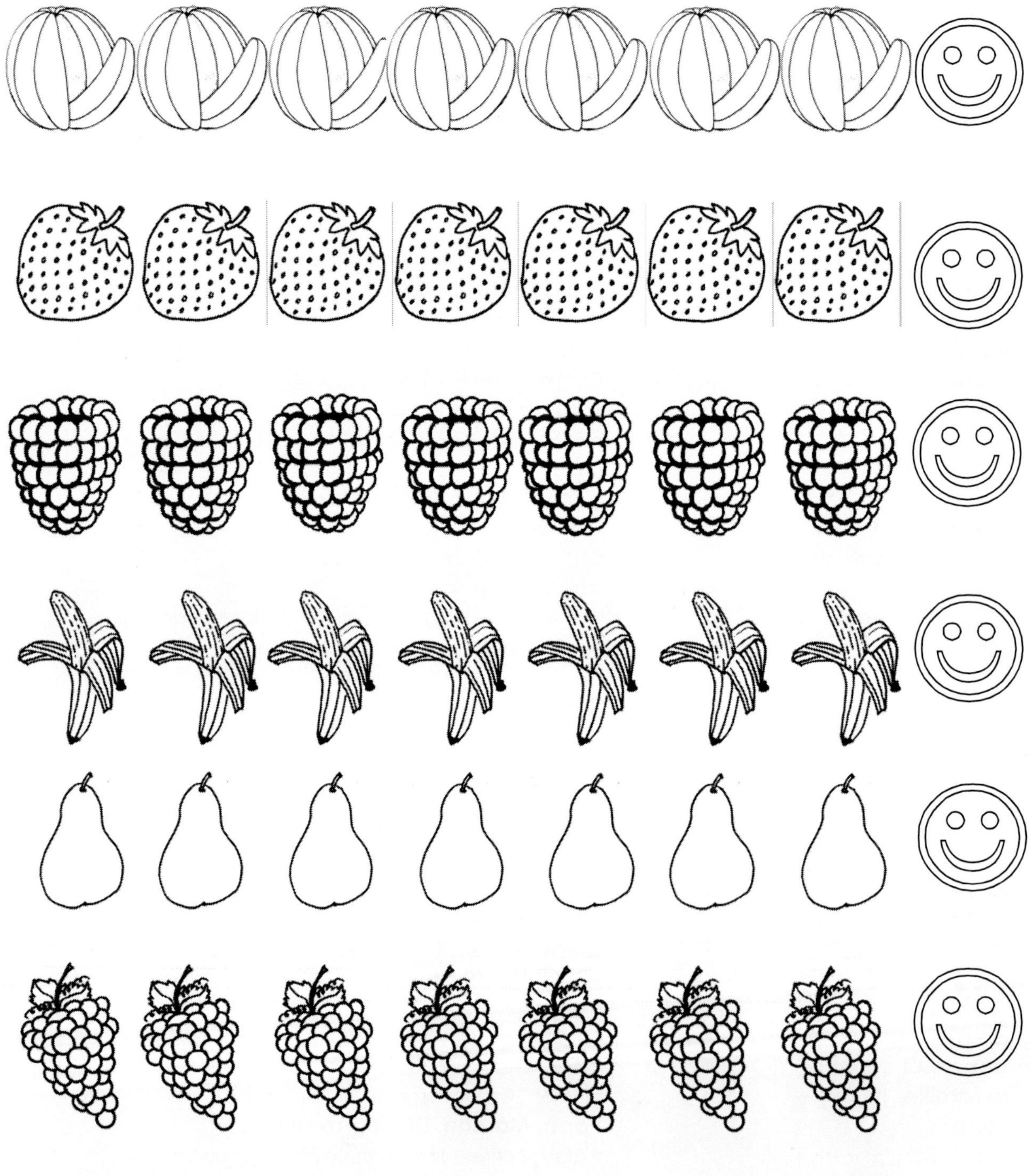

Page 1 'les couleurs (i)' - colours

Page 1:1

Listen to the CD

The children are introduced to five colours in French.

Each colour is written, in French, and has its colour coded picture.

Three colours are used here including white (which is not mentioned in the pupil's book)

THE LESSON: Hand out the worksheets and go over the colours with the children. (Use the felt squares to illustrate the colours)

Call out some English words which have a strong colour association and get the children to give you the French colour.
eg lemon (jaune) strawberry (rouge) leaf (vert) etc

CD Script

Colorie (Colour) **le drapeau** (flag) **de l'Angleterre en blanc et rouge.**
Colorie le drapeau de la France en bleu, rouge et blanc.
Colorie le drapeau de l'Espagne (Spain) **en rouge et jaune.**

Page 1:2

Write the colours

Écris les couleurs – Write the colours

Any worksheet with **:2** after its page number is for children who find writing easy and need stretching.

Here they need to colour the images at the top of the page in their correct colour and then write the French for each appropriate colour next to the pictures down the side of the page.

eg daffodil - **jaune** ladybird - **rouge** leaf - **vert** etc

Page 1:3

Association in French

Colorie les ballons – Colour the balloons

Colour each teddy's tee-shirt in the correct colour.
There are colour clues to help the early readers.

Make sure each teddy's balloon is coloured the same colour as its tee-shirt.

The felt colour game

As-tu le bleu? Have you got the blue?

Children sit in a circle

Take six coloured felt squares (blue, red, white, yellow, pink and green)
Whilst singing 'Frère Jacques' (See page 3) get the children to pass the felts round in a circle.
On the last word of the song (dong) the children with the felt squares sit on them (the others pretend to do the same).
Children take it in turns to ask each other "As-tu le (whatever colour)?" until the correct child has been asked.
Keep going until all the colours have been discovered.
TIP Write all the colours used on the board.
As they are discovered, tick them off so the children can see what colours have been mentioned.

Mon nom ....

Complète et colorie les drapeaux

Complete and colour the flags

Angleterre

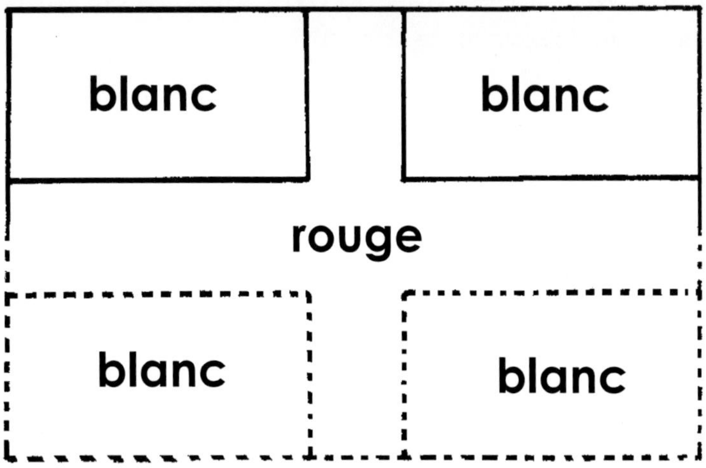

blanc rouge

France

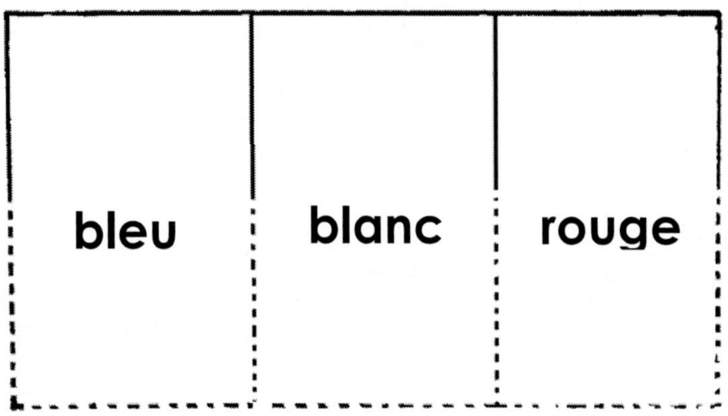

bleu rouge blanc

Espagne

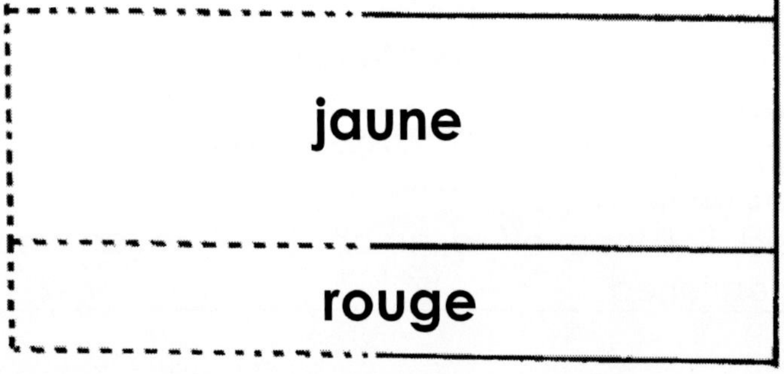

rouge jaune

Mon nom ....

Écris les couleurs

Write the colours

rouge **jaune** **vert** **bleu** **rose**

....

....

....

....

....

....

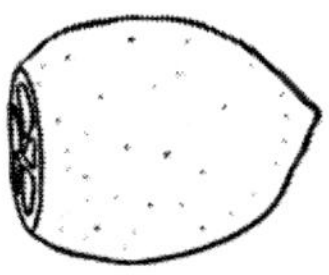
....

....

Mon nom ....

Colorie les ballons

Colour the balloons

rouge **vert** **jaune** **rose** **bleu**

Page 2 'les couleurs (ii)' - colours

Page 2 :1

Listen to the CD

Entoure la bonne couleur – Circle the correct colour

The children are introduced to five more colours in French.

Each colour is written, in French, and has its colour coded picture.

THE LESSON: Hand out the worksheets and go over the colours with the children. (Use the felt squares to illustrate the colours)
Call out some English words which have a strong colour association and get the children to give you the French colour.
eg chocolate (marron) carrot (orange) elephant (grey) etc

LISTEN TO THE CD

Entoure le mot orange. Circle the word orange.	**Entoure le mot violet.** Circle the word purple.
Entoure le mot jaune.	**Entoure le mot gris.**
Entoure le mot blanc.	**Entoure le mot noir.**
Entoure le mot marron.	**Entoure le mot bleu.**
Entoure le mot rouge.	**Entoure le mot vert.**

Page 2 :2

Observe and colour in French

Colorie les images – Colour the pictures

This is a straight forward colouring exercise.

Here they need to colour the images in their correct colour.

Colour coded pictures have also been given.

eg carrot - **orange** thistle - **purple** snowman - **white**

Page 2 :3

Craft in French

les couleurs – Colour cube

This is a craft activity to make a colour cube.

Colour in the squares according to the pictures.

Cut out the whole shape and fold over the dotted line flaps.
Stick/staple together, if necessary.

When the cubes are finished you can play a game.

The colour cube game

The colour cube game

Call out a colour, for example, **rouge**.

The children throw their colour cubes and whoever throws a **rouge** wins the round.

This game can be played several times but not for long as the children will get bored.

If you have list of all the children in the class you could tick the name of each winner and give a star to the first child to win the game three times.

Mon nom ....

Écoute et entoure la bonne couleur

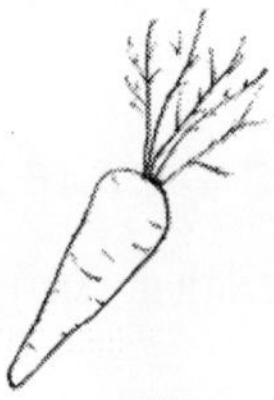	orange	jaune	vert
	bleu	rouge	violet
	rose	jaune	noir
	bleu	orange	gris
	violet	blanc	noir
	noir	vert	jaune
	bleu	rouge	marron
	rose	bleu	orange
	gris	rouge	vert
	noir	jaune	vert

Mon nom ....

Colorie les images

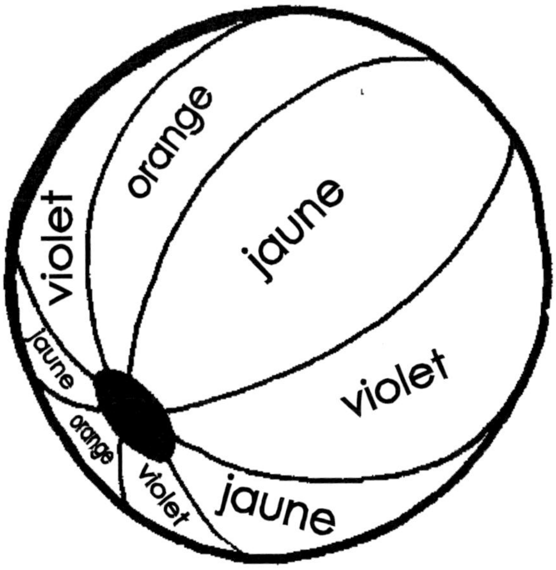

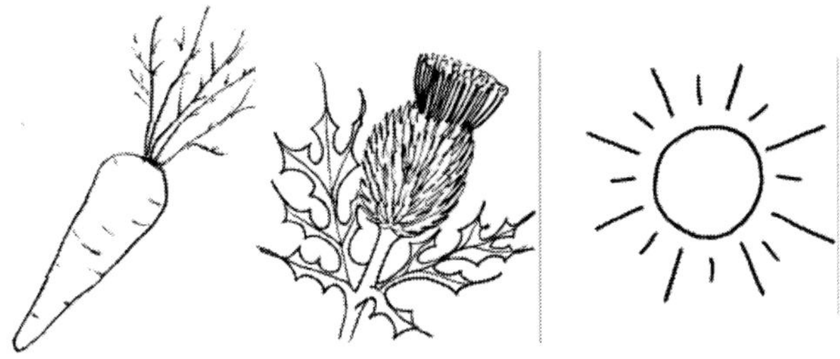

orange violet jaune

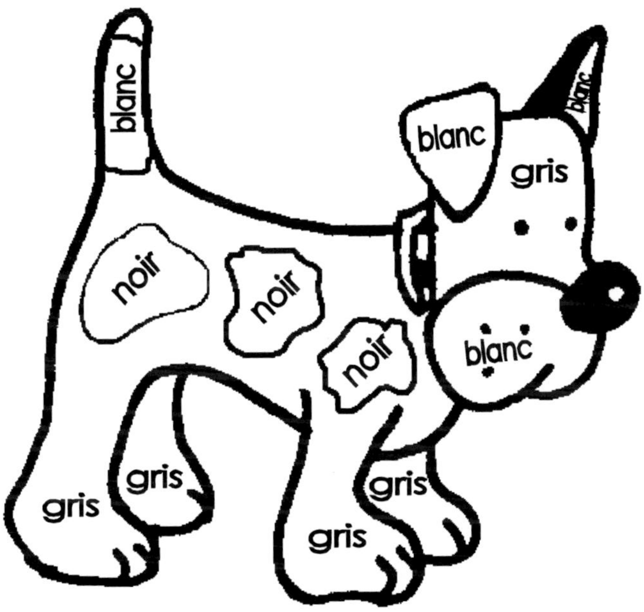

gris noir blanc

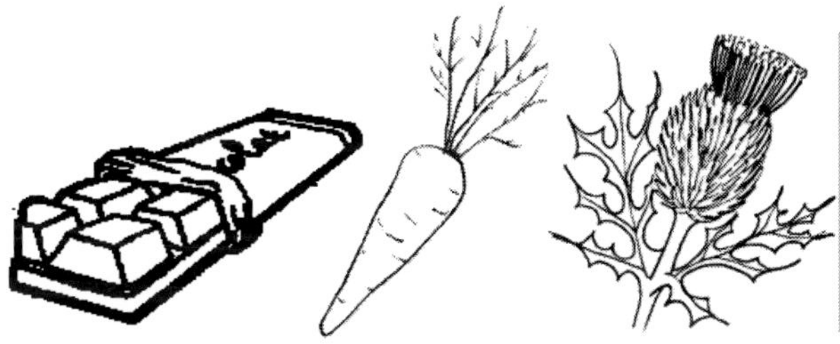

marron orange violet

les couleurs

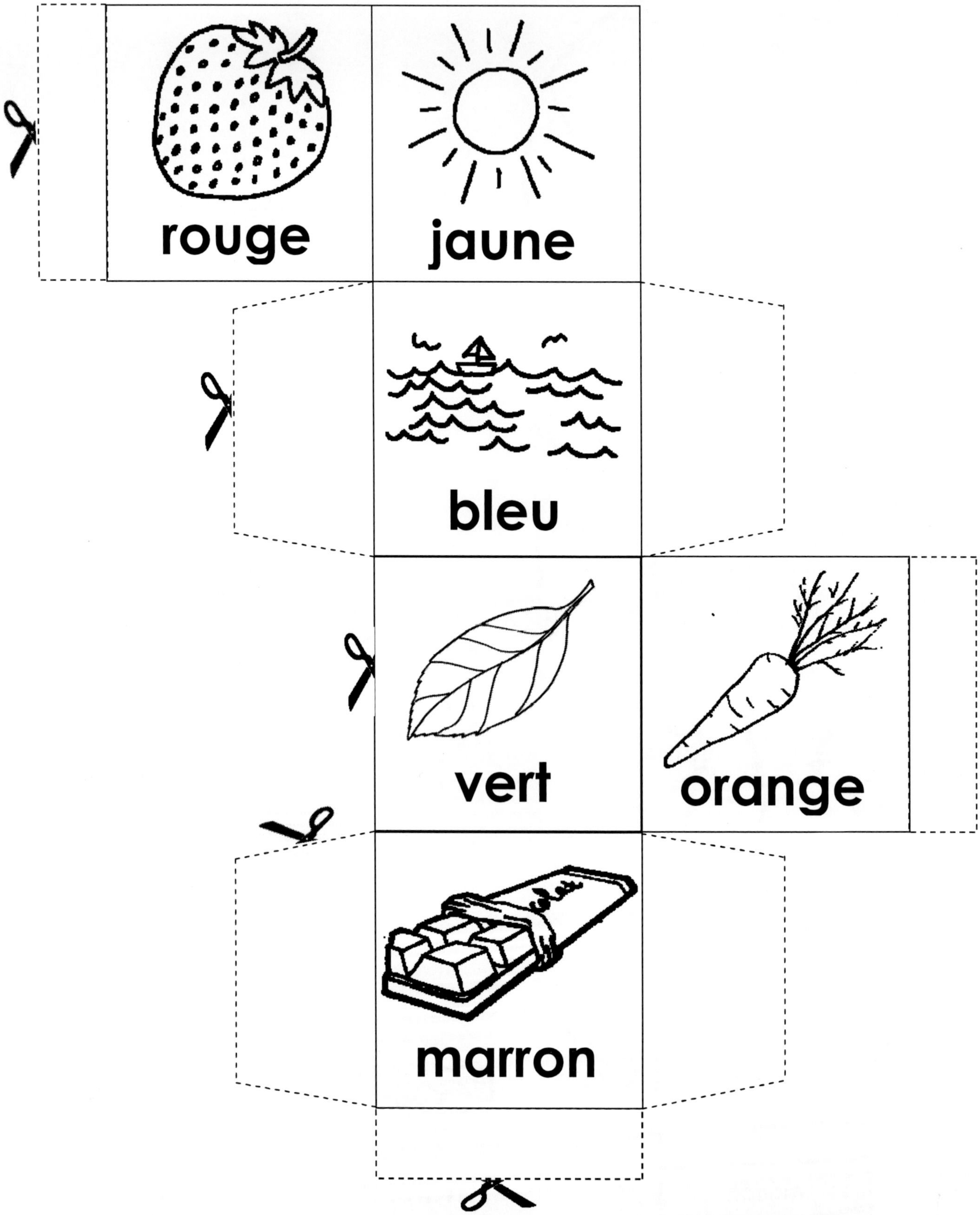

Frère Jacques

Frère Jacques Frère Jacques
Dormez-vous? Dormez-vous?

Sonnez les matines
Sonnez les matines
Ding dang dong
Ding dang dong

3:1 (Track 54 karaoke version)

Mon nom ....

Compte et colorie les cloches

Count and colour the bells

1. Colorie deux 2 **cloches** en violet. 

2. Colorie cinq 5 **cloches** en orange. 

3. Colorie une 1 **cloche** en gris. 

4. Colorie quatre 4 **cloches** en rouge. 

5. Colorie trois 3 **cloches** en marron. 

Page 4 'les nombres (i)' - numbers

Page 4 :1

Count the sweets Listen to the CD

Compte et colorie les bonbons – Count and colour the sweets

On this page the children learn to count and colour.

Go over the numbers from 1 – 5 in French and the five colours.

Count aloud with the fingers of one hand.

Sometimes it is useful to count backwards in French to make sure the children know their numbers thoroughly.

LISTEN TO THE CD

Colorie un bonbon en orange.	Colour one sweet orange.
Colorie deux bonbons en rouge.	Colour two sweets red.
Colorie trois bonbons en jaune.	Colour three sweets yellow.
Colorie quatre bonbons en bleu.	Colour four sweets blue.
Colorie cinq bonbons en vert.	Colour five sweets green.

Page 4 :2

Maths in French

Compte, calcule et écris – Count, work out and write

deux	plus	trois	égalent	cinq	two plus three equals five
un	plus	un	égalent	deux	one plus one equals two
deux	plus	un	égalent	trois	two plus one equals three
deux	plus	zéro	égalent	deux	two plus naught equals two
deux	plus	deux	égalent	quatre	two plus two equals four
deux	plus	trois	égalent	cinq	two plus three equals five

Page 4 :3

Observe in French

Compte les moutons – Count the sheep

This exercise is fine for those children who find writing easy.
If they enjoy colouring they can complete the picture.

The felt colour game

As-tu le bleu? Have you got the blue? Children sit in a circle

Take six coloured felt squares (blue, red, white, yellow, pink and green)

Whilst singing '**Frère Jacques**' (See page 3) get the children to pass the felts round in a circle.
On the last word of the song (dong) the children with the felt squares sit on them (the others pretend to do the same).
Children take it in turns to ask each other "As-tu le (whatever colour)?" until the correct child has been asked.
Keep going until all the colours have been discovered.
TIP Write all the colours used on the white board. As they are discovered, tick them off so the children can see what colours have been mentioned.

Mon nom ....

Compte et colorie

Count and colour

1	2	3	4	5
un	deux	trois	quatre	cinq

orange	rouge	jaune	bleu	vert

Mon nom ....

Compte, calcule et écris

1	2	3	4	5
un	deux	trois	quatre	cinq

deux + trois = cinq

un + un = ...

deux + un = ...

deux + zéro = ...

deux + deux = ...

deux + trois = ...

Mon nom ....

Compte les moutons

Look at the sheep's legs then write the correct number of sheep matching the examples.

1	2	3	4	5
un	deux	trois	quatre	cinq

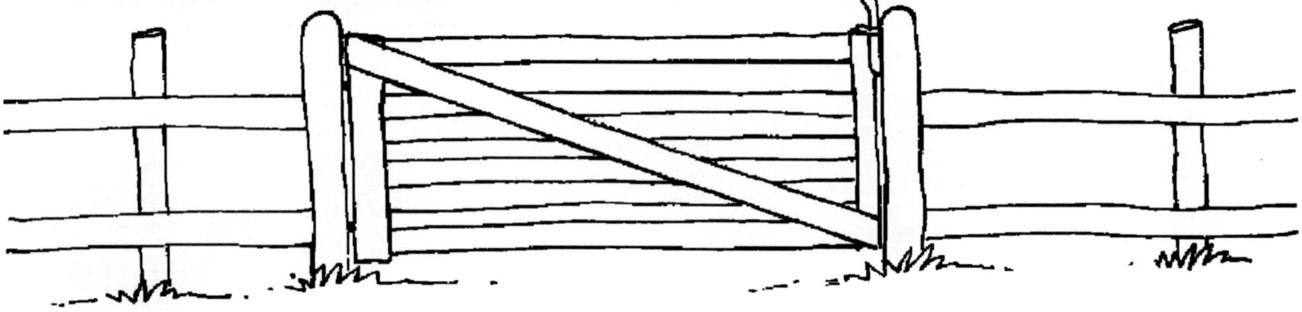

....

....

....

....

....

Page 5 'les nombres (ii)' - numbers

Page 5 :1

Colorie l'image

Listen to the CD

Colorie l'image – Colour the picture

Revise numbers 1 – 10 and colours
Sometimes it is useful to count backwards in French to make sure the children know their numbers thoroughly.

LISTEN TO THE CD

Colorie un en bleu.	Colour one blue.
Colorie deux en jaune.	Colour two yellow.
Colorie trois en marron.	Colour three brown.
Colorie quatre en vert.	Colour four green.
Colorie cinq en rose.	Colour five pink.
Colorie six en noir.	Colour six black.
Colorie sept en rouge.	Colour seven red.
Colorie huit en violet.	Colour eight purple.

Page 5 :2

Observe in French

Compte et colorie – Count and colour

This exercise is fine for those children who find writing easy.

If they enjoy colouring they can complete the picture.

The more able children could write the colours they have chosen next to each fruit and vegetable.

Page 5 :3

Maths in French

Compte et colorie – Count and colour

Look at the numbers at the bottom of each column of fruit.
Colour in that exact number of fruit.

(apples)	eight	(strawberries)	ten
(lemons)	nine	(raspberries)	six
(pears)	seven		

Song

Frère Jacques

Frère Jacques

Practise singing this song and make sure the picture (3:1) and the acitivity (3:2) have been completed.

If the children know the song particularly well, you can try and sing it as a round. The music enables you to sing it three times.

Revision

Colours

Revision

Revise all the colours that have been covered in the first three chapters of the book by holding up the felt squares one at a time to see if the children can remember the French for each colour.

If a child remembers the colour, he can keep the felt and then come to the front and hold up his felt to revise the colours again.

Mon nom ....

Colorie l'image

1  **bleu**

2  **jaune**

3  **marron**

4  **vert**

5  **rose**

6  **noir**

7  **rouge**

8  **violet**

Mon nom ....

Compte et colorie.

2	3	4	5	6	7	8	9
deux	trois	quatre	cinq	six	sept	huit	neuf

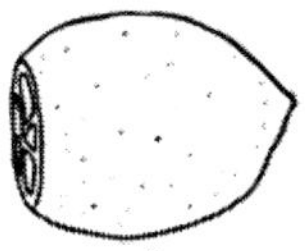 ......**deux**......

 ....

 ....

 ....

 ....

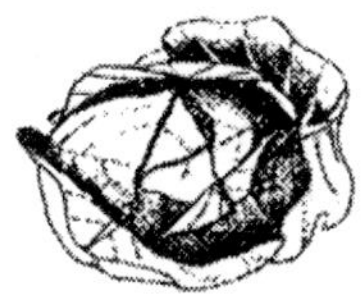 ....

 ....

 ....

Mon nom ....

Compte et colorie.

6	7	8	9	10
six	sept	huit	neuf	dix

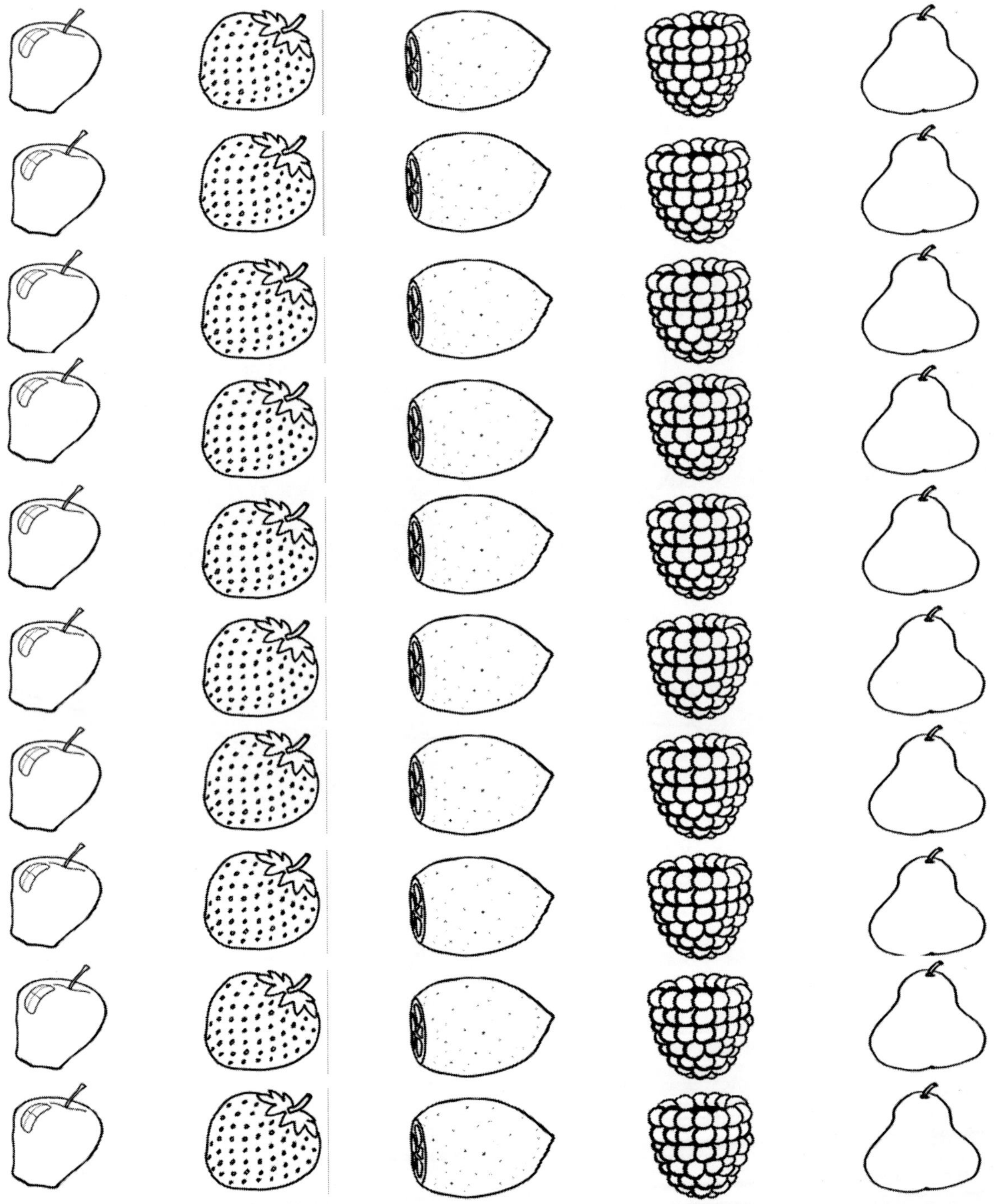

huit dix neuf six sept

Page 6 'Présent ! Présente !' - present

Page 6 :1

Présent! Présente!

Listen to the CD

Présent! Présente! – present (as in taking the school register)

Take the class's register in French.
The boys need to reply **present** (Do not pronounce the T)
The girls need to reply **présente** (Pronounce the T)

LISTEN TO THE CD

Emilie **présente**
Sophie **présente**
Patrice **présent**
Gilbert **présent**
Hubert **présent**

Page 6 :2

Observe in French

Présent! Présente! – present (as in taking the school register)

Look at the page and work out how many boys are present in the class and how many girls.

Write the answer in full at the bottom of the page.

Page 6 :3

Spot the difference

Trouve les 10 différences – Spot the 10 differences

1. The letter A on the wall.
2. The tip of the dog's nose
3. The two books on the floor
4. The three books on the shelf
5. The elephant's eye
6. The mouse's ears
7. The giraffe's spots
8. The guitar on the shelf
9. The octopus' cap
10. The octopus' leg

Song

Frère Jacques

Frère Jacques

Practise singing this song and make sure the picture (3:1) and the acitivity (3:2) have been completed.

If the children know the song particularly well you can try and sing it as a round.

Revision

Colours

Revision

Revise all the colours that have been covered in the first three chapters of the book by holding up the felt squares one at a time to see if the children can remember the French for each colour.

If a child remembers the colour, he can keep the felt and then come to the front and hold up his felt to revise the colours again.

Mon nom ....

Présent, Présente

Mon nom ....

Présent! Présente!

Count the number of girls and boys present ✓ in the class and write each number in the box and on the line at the bottom of the page.

4	5	6	7	8
quatre	**cinq**	**six**	**sept**	**huit**

Présent  ☐ ....

Présente  ☐ ....

Mon nom ....

Trouve les 10 différences

un oiseau, deux oiseaux

un oiseau
deux oiseaux
sur la plage sur la plage

un seau d'eau
deux seaux d'eau
sur la plage sur la plage

un château
deux châteaux
sur la plage sur la plage

un bateau
deux bateaux
sur la plage sur la plage

Repeat 1st verse

Mon nom ....

Colorie l'image

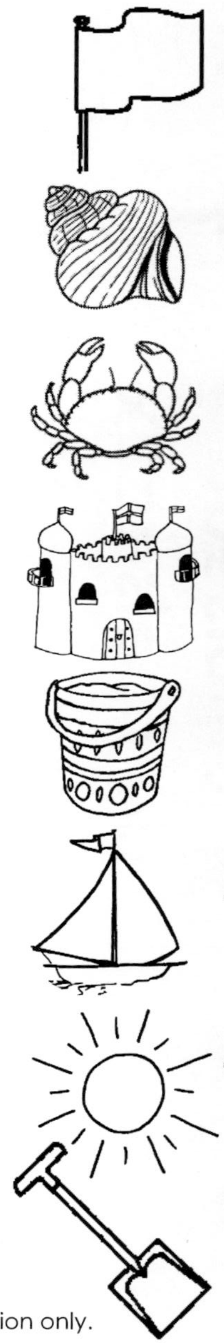

violet

rouge

rose

orange

vert

jaune

jaune

bleu

Page 8 'un jeu' – a game

Page 8 :1

un jeu

Listen to the CD

un jeu – a game

This is a whole class listening exercise.

1. Go over all the colours (following the symbols) with the class.
   leaf (vert) carrot (orange) thistle (violet) chocolate (marron)
   Each of the 9 boxes is a different colour.
2. Revise numbers 1 – 10
3. Colour the boxes **(NOT THE SMALL MIDDLE BOXES)** in their correct c olours.

CD Script

Écris le numéro **un** dans le carré **gris**.
Write the number one in the grey square.
Écris le numéro **deux** dans le carré **bleu**.
Write the number two in the blue square.
Écris le numéro **trois** dans le carré **jaune**.
Write the number three in the yellow square.
Écris le numéro **quatre** dans le carré **orange**.
Write the number four in the orange square.
Écris le numéro **cinq** dans le carré **marron**.
Write the number five in the brown square.
Écris le numéro **six** dans le carré **rouge**.
Write the number six in the red square.
Écris le numéro **sept** dans le carré **violet**.
Write the number seven in the purple square.
Écris le numéro **huit** dans le carré **rose**.
Write the number huit in the pink square.

Page 8 :2

Observe and count in French

Compte et colorie les carrés – Count and colour the squares

This revision exercise can be completed by children of all levels.
Even the poor readers should be able to complete the task

Revise the vocabulary with the children before starting the worksheet.
Colorie colour le carré square

This exercise appears to be difficult but it isn't.
Look at the **number** and the **colour symbol** on each line.
Colour that number of squares in the correct colour.

End of lesson

Songs
Felt game
Revision

SONG Frère Jacques (3 :1)
SONG un oiseau, deux oiseaux (7 :1)

If there is time at the end of this lesson you can choose one of the following activities:

1. Sing **Frère Jacques,**
2. Sing **un oiseau, deux oiseaux**
3. Play the felt game.
4. Take the class register (remember **present** and **présente**)

Mon nom ....

un jeu

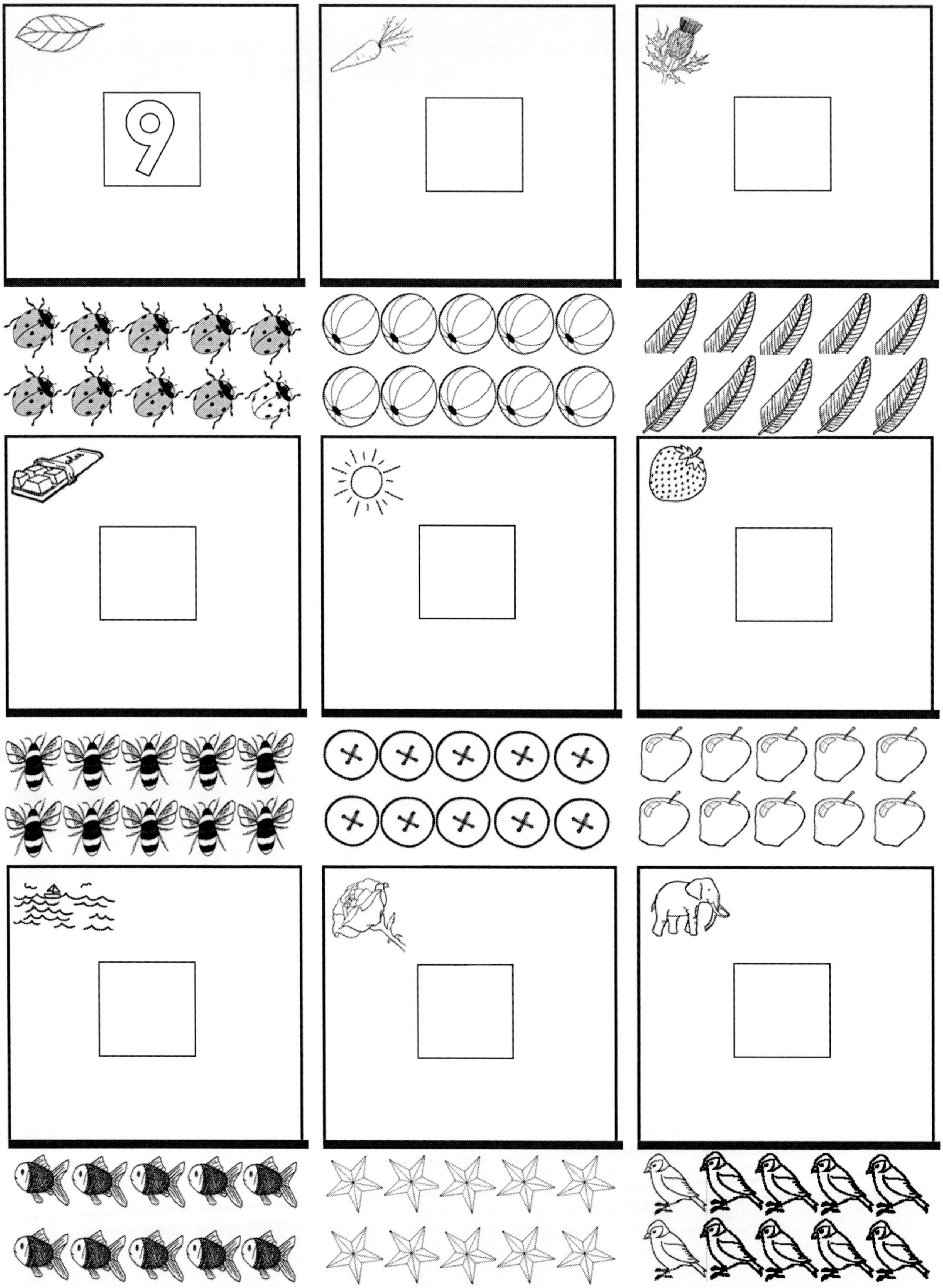

Mon nom ....

Compte et colorie les carrés

Count and colour the squares

1. Colorie deux 2 **carrés** en jaune. 

2. Colorie cinq 5 **carrés** en vert. 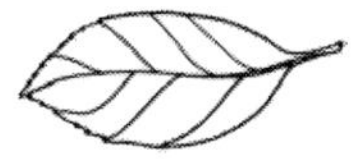

3. Colorie un 1 **carré** en bleu. 

4. Colorie quatre 4 **carrés** en rouge. 

5. Colorie trois 3 **carrés** en orange. 

Page 9 'les révisions' – revision

Page 9 :1

Count & colour

Listen to the CD

Écoute et colorie – Listen and colour

This is a whole class activity and listening exercise.

1. Go over all 10 colours (use the felts for their visual effects)
2. Revise numbers 1 – 10 Try and vary the counting by counting backwards, counting the even **(pair)** numbers and then the odd **(impair)** numbers
3. Colour/circle the words and pictures in their correct colours.

CD Script

Colorie cinq en violet.	Colour (picture number) five in purple.
Colorie un en bleu.	Colour one in blue.
Colorie sept en marron.	Colour sept in brown.
Colorie quatre en jaune.	Colour four in yellow.
Colorie huit en orange.	Colour eight in orange.
Colorie deux en rouge.	Colour two in red.
Colorie six en vert.	Colour six in green.
Colorie trois en rose.	Colour three in pink.
Colorie dix en blanc.	Colour ten in white.
Colorie neuf en gris.	Colour nine in grey.

Page 9 :2

Observe and count in French

loto– bingo

NB When photocopying make sure the teacher has a copy so he/she can tick off the colours and numbers as a reference.

This is a revision exercise for numbers 1 – 10 and colours.
Everyone can play, even the poor readers, because all the colours are in symbol form (no reading is required).

1st game: Ask the children to colour in 5 numbers.

Start reading out the numbers very slowly.
The children cross out the numbers they have coloured.

The winner is the first child to cross out all 5 pictures.
This game can be played four times.

Page 9 :3

Dice game in French

Jeu de dé – dice game

This is a whole class activity.

1. Ask the children to fold their piece of paper in half so only one picture can be seen.
2. Colour in the six little boxes marked 1 – 6 in their correct colours.
3. The teacher throws a dice and calls out the number.

   The children colour in that part of the picture.
   Continue until all the numbered parts of the picture have been coloured in.

Mon nom ....

Écoute et colorie

1	2	3	4	5
bleu	rouge	rose	jaune	violet
6	7	8	9	10
vert	marron	orange	gris	blanc

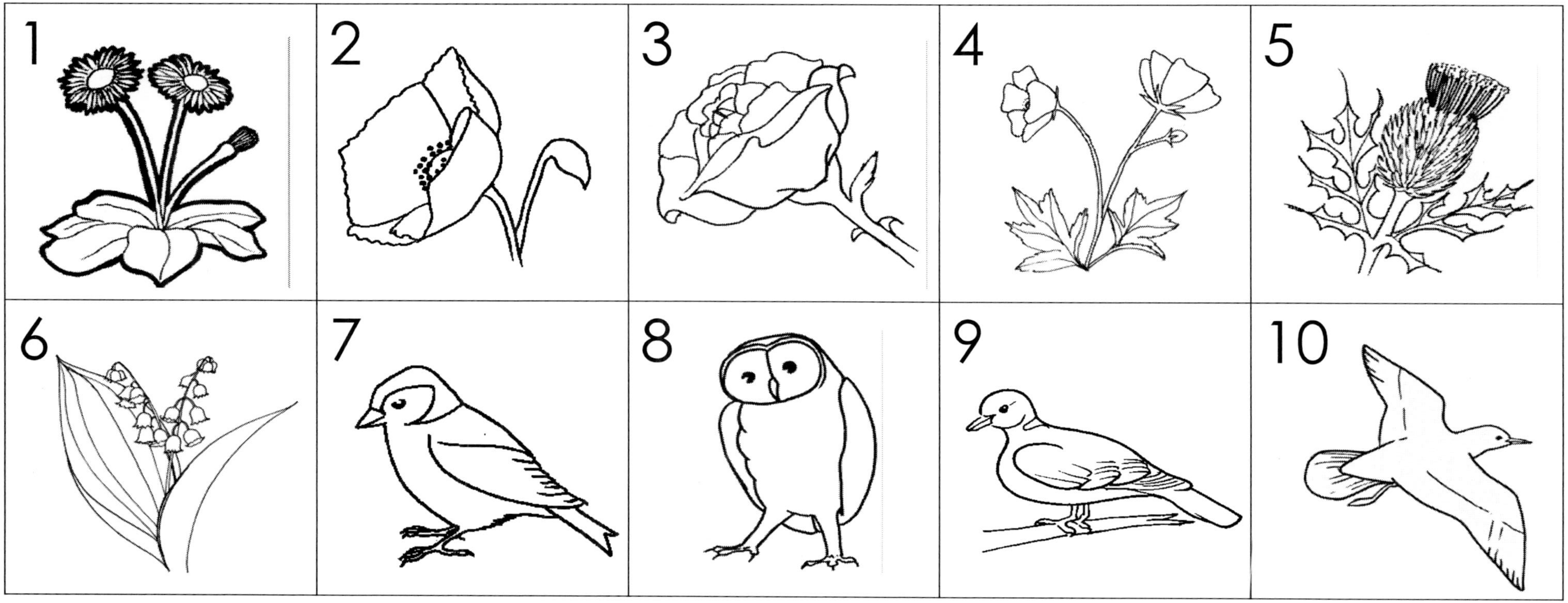

Mon nom ....

loto

1	2	3	4	5	6	7	8	9	10
un	deux	trois	quatre	cinq	six	sept	huit	neuf	dix

jaune bleu vert marron blanc rouge orange violet noir rose

1	2	3	4	5	6	7	8	9	10
un	deux	trois	quatre	cinq	six	sept	huit	neuf	dix

jaune bleu vert marron blanc rouge orange violet noir rose

Mon nom ....

jeu de dé

1	bleu
2	jaune
3	orange
4	violet
5	vert
6	rouge

1	bleu
2	jaune
3	orange
4	violet
5	vert
6	rouge

Cinq petits vers

1 2 3 4 5 vers 5 petits vers
1 2 3 4 5 vers dans la terre

1 2 3 4 vers 4 petits vers
1 2 3 4 vers dans la terre

1 2 3 vers 3 petits vers
1 2 3 vers dans la terre

1 2 vers 2 petits vers
1 2 vers dans la terre

Un petit ver sans ami
Un petit ver sans ami dans la terre

10:1 (Track 56 Karaoke version)

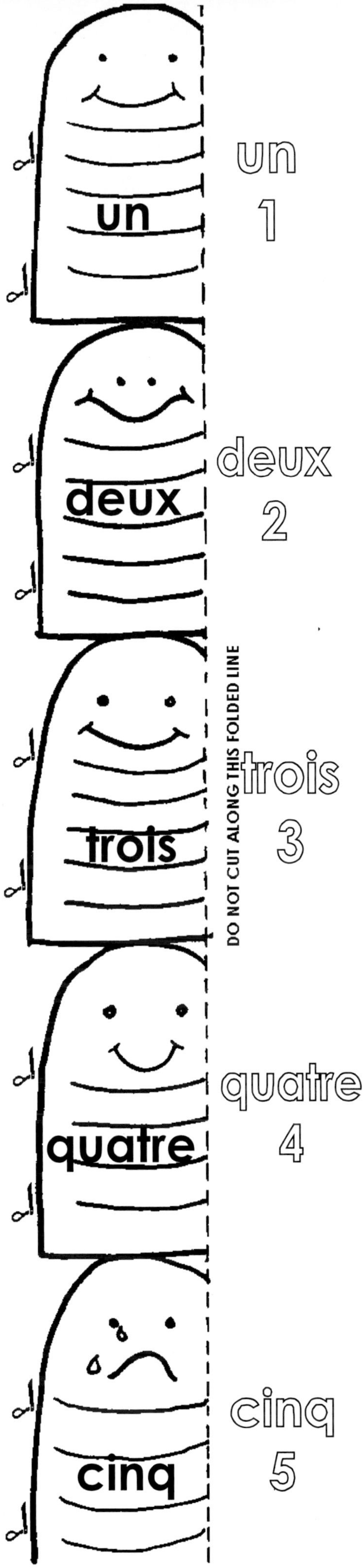

These are finger puppets to go with the song 'Cinq Petits Vers'

Fold the paper along the dotted line and cut round each little worm.

Once folded the worms can be 'sellotaped' or stapled into position.

Page 11 'les vêtements (i)' - clothes

Page 11 :1

Beware of the cauliflowers!

Listen to the CD

Attention aux choux-fleurs! – Beware of the cauliflowers!

This is a dice game.
Fold the paper along the dotted line. One side for each game.

The teacher throws a dice and reads out the number followed by the French for the picture in the box.

The aim of the game is to colour in (very quickly) all five pictures before three 6s (the cauliflowers) have been thrown.

CD Script (If you do not wish to play with a dice)

Game 1: You lose

trois la jupe	**deux la robe**	**cinq le jean**	**un la chemise**
trois la jupe	**six le chou-fleur**	**cinq le jean**	**six le chou-fleur**
un la chemise	**deux la robe**	**trois la jupe**	**six le chou-fleur**

Game 2: You win

un la chemise	**quatre le pull**	**six le chou-fleur**	**un la chemise**
trois la jupe	**six le chou-fleur**	**deux la robe**	**quatre le pull**
deux la robe	**trois la jupe**	**trois la jupe**	**cinq le jean**

Page 11 :2

Co-ordinates in French

Dessine dans les carrés – Draw in the squares

This exercise is fine for children who find writing easy and understand the concept of co-ordinates.

The drawings and writing should be neatly done.

Page 11 :3

Craft in French

Craft

1. Go over the items of clothing with the children.
2. Ask the children to colour in one top and one bottom.
3. Cut out the figure of the child and stick it onto sugar paper.
4. Cut out the coloured items of clothing and stick them onto the figure of the child.
5. The confident writers can label their picture.

IDEAL FOR CLASSROOM DISPLAY

The felt colour game

Game Children stand in a circle

Put 10 coloured felt squares neatly in the centre of the circle.
One child stands in the middle of the circle.
Whilst singing '**Frère Jacques**' the other children walk **SLOWLY** round in a circle (holding hands) but facing outwards and the child in the middle takes one felt square and sits on it so it is hidden.
On the last word of the song (dong) the children in the circle jump round facing inwards and sit down.

They have to guess which colour the child in the middle is hiding.

Mon nom ....

Attention aux choux-fleurs!

Mon nom ....

Dessine dans les carrés

	a	b	c
1			
2			
3			

le pull 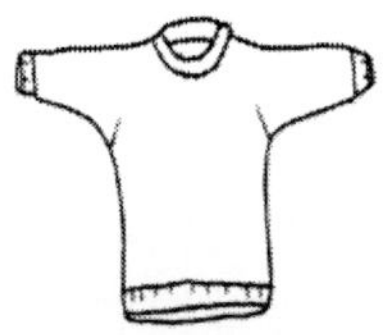 3 a

....

le jean  1 b

....

la jupe  3 c

....

la chemise  2 a

....

la robe  1 c

....

le pull

la jupe

le jean

la chemise

Page 12 'les vêtements (ii)' - clothes

Page 12 :1

How much is it?

Listen to the CD

C'est combien? – How much is it?

This is a whole class listening and number exercise.

Listen to the CD and write on the dotted lines the number which goes with each item of clothing (either in word or number form).

CD Script

Les baskets coûtent dix (10) euros.
The trainers cost ten euros.

Le tee-shirt coûte trois (3) euros.
The tee-shirt costs three euros.

Les chaussures coûtent neuf (9) euros.
The shoes cost nine euros.

Le pantalon coûte huit (8) euros.
The trousers cost eight euros.

Les chaussettes coûtent deux (2) euros.
The socks cost two euros.

Page 12 :2

Find the odd one out

Trouve l'intrus – Find the odd one out

This exercise is for the children who find writing easy.

All they have to do is circle the odd picture in each line and then write its French name on the dotted line.

All worksheets marked **:2** should be completed neatly and accurately.

Page 12 :3

Word recognition and sounds

Entoure le bon mot - Circle the correct word.

This can be done as a whole class activity or individually.

1. Go over the items of clothing on the washing line revising the vocabulary..
2. The children circle the correct word for each garment.
3. If the children cannot read, the teacher reads out the choice of two words and the children listen and then circle the correct word based on the initial letter sound or memory.

(Don't forget that the letters **CH** in French are pronounced **SH**)

Page 20

Song

Je vois deux chaussettes

Je vois deux chaussettes I can see two socks

This song revises some clothing words in French.

Get the children to point to the pictures as the song is sung.

A black and white picture is found on page 20:1 if you want the children to colour in the song sheet.

If you wish to complete the craft activity at this stage, it is found on worksheet 20:2

Mon nom ....

C'est combien?

Les baskets coûtent ....€

Le tee-shirt coûte ....€

Les chaussures coûtent ....€

Le pantalon coûte ....€

Les chaussettes coûtent ....€

Mon nom ....

Trouve l'intrus

 le **tee-shirt**

 la **chaussure**

 la **basket**

 la **chaussette**

 le **pantalon**

le ....

le ....

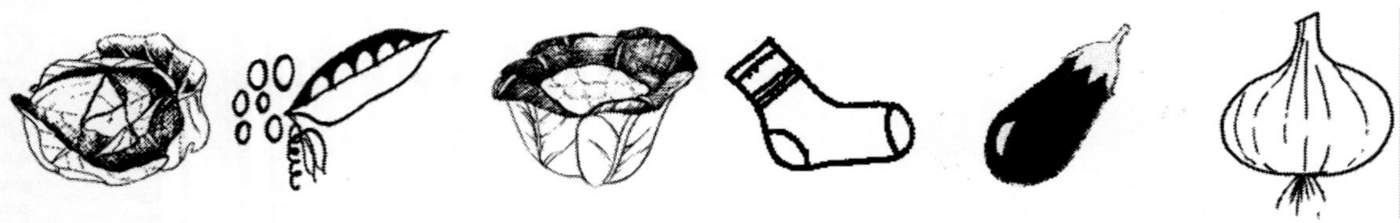

la ....

la ....

la ....

Mon nom ....

Entoure le bon mot

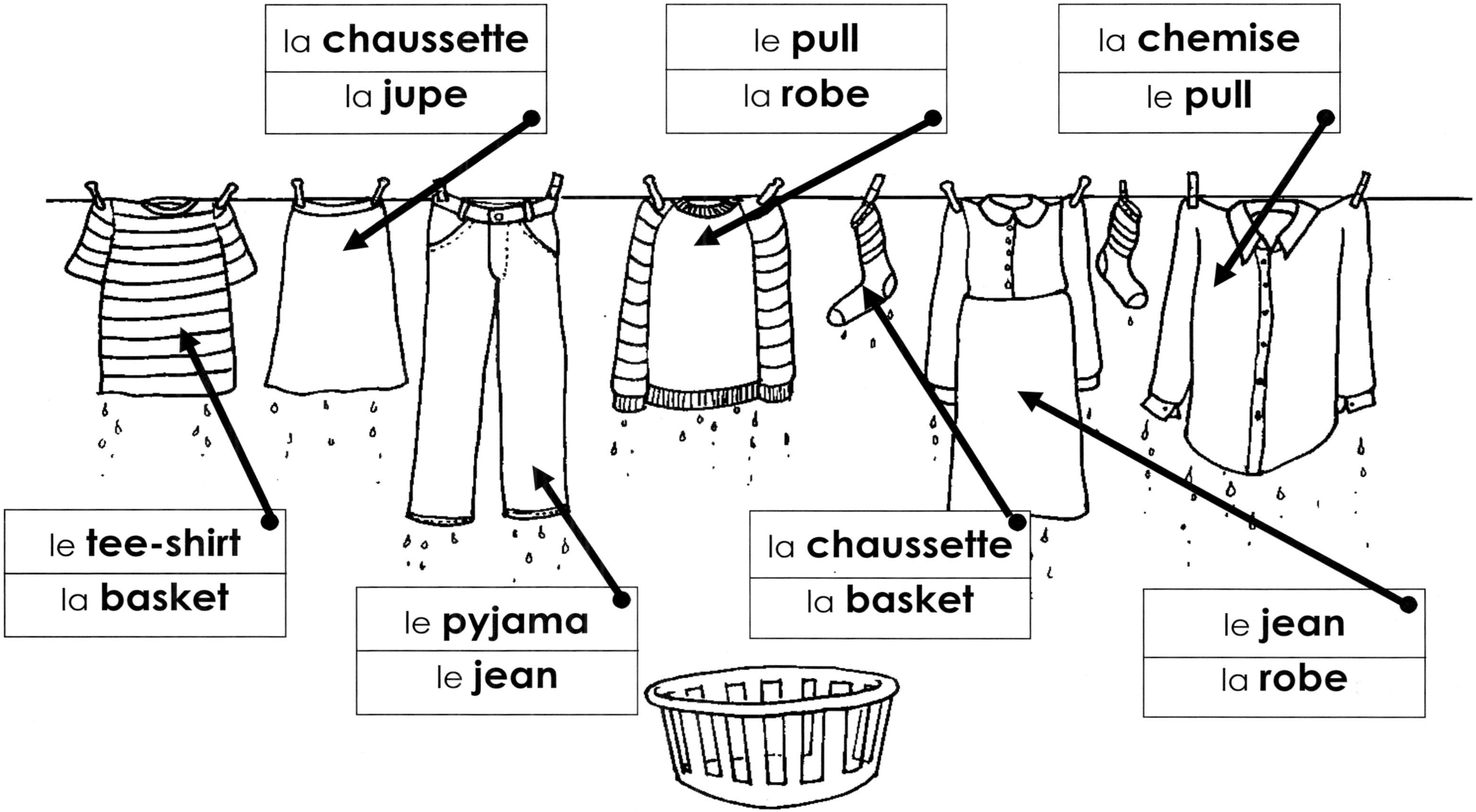

Où est le grand lion?

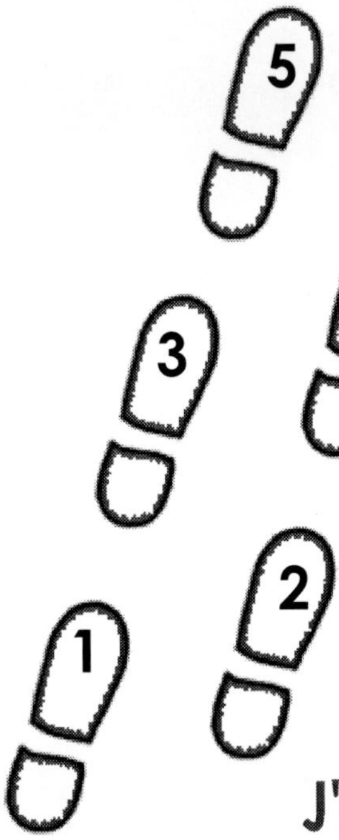

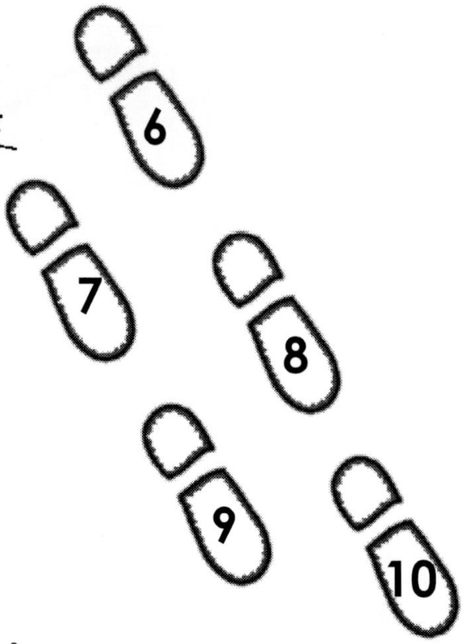

1 2 3 4 5 petits pas
Où est le grand lion?
6 7 8 9 10 petits pas
Où est le grand lion?

J'ai peur, j'ai peur, j'ai peur, j'ai peur
J'ai peur du grand lion
J'ai peur, j'ai peur, j'ai peur, j'ai peur
J'ai peur du grand lion

1 2 3 4 5 petits pas
Je vois le grand lion
6 7 8 9 10 petits pas
Je vois le grand lion

J'ai peur, j'ai peur, j'ai peur, j'ai peur
J'ai peur du grand lion
J'ai peur, j'ai peur, j'ai peur, j'ai peur
J'ai peur du grand lion

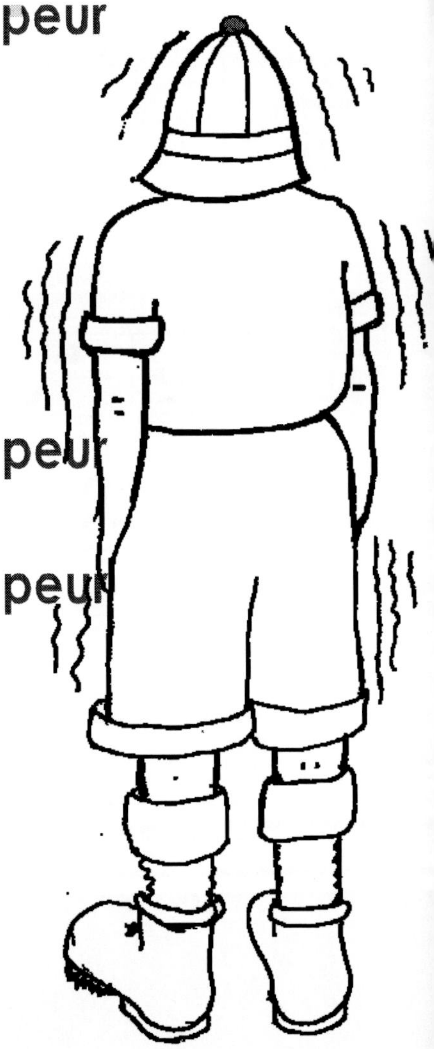

Où est le grand lion?

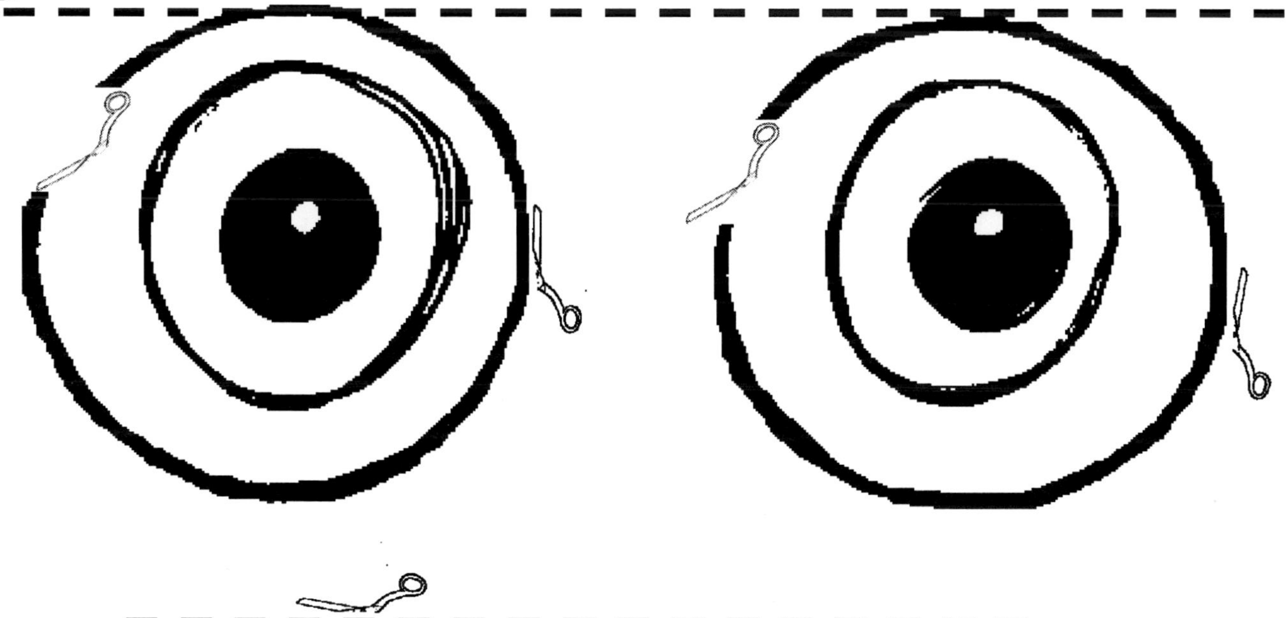

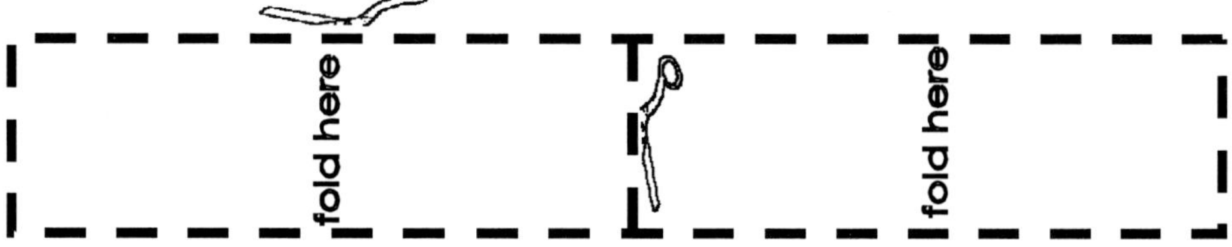

Page 14 'J'ai faim (i)' – I'm hungry

Page 14 :1

Listen carefully

Listen to the CD

Ecoute bien et écris les chiffres – Listen carefully and write the numbers

This is a whole class listening and number exercise.

Listen to the CD and write the correct number in each box.
The numbers are not in order to stop the children rushing ahead.

CD Script

Le beurre est numéro sept.
The butter is number seven.

Le lait est numéro dix.
The milk is number ten.

La confiture est numéro neuf.
The jam is number nine.

Le pain est numéro six.
The bread is number six.

Le fromage est numéro huit.
The cheese is number eight.

Page 14 :2

Word search

J'ai faim – I'm hungry

This worksheet can be used for both able writers and early learners.

1. The able writers need to copy the words on the dotted lines.
2. The less fluent writers need only find the words in the wordsearch.

For children who enjoy colouring, each word in the wordsearch can be coloured separately.
All worksheets marked **:2** should be completed neatly and accurately.

Page 14 :3

Maths in French

Compte, calcule et écris – Count, calculate and write.

This is a maths paper which can be used for both able writers and early learners.

Remind the children that these are subtraction sums.

1. The confident writers count the crabs, write the number and calculate the sum, writing the answer in the large crab.
2. The less confident writers need only work out the sum and write the answer in the large crab.

Songs

Pages

3, 7, 10, 13 and 20

Songs

By now the children will have come across five songs.

Make sure all the song sheets have been coloured in and completed.

Perhaps the children who have helped clear the tables could choose which song they wish to sing.

Mon nom ....

Écoute bien et écris les chiffres

6	7	8	9	10
six	**sept**	**huit**	**neuf**	**dix**

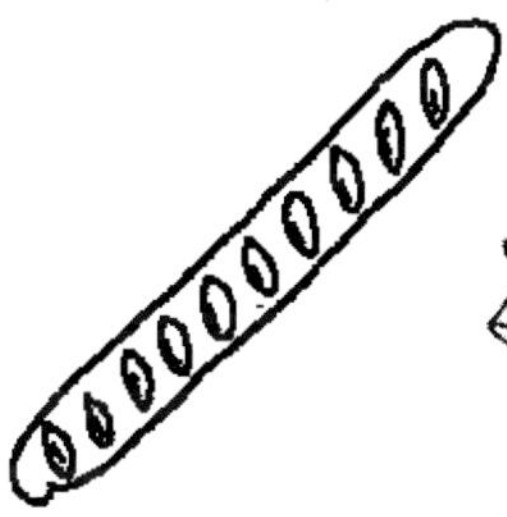

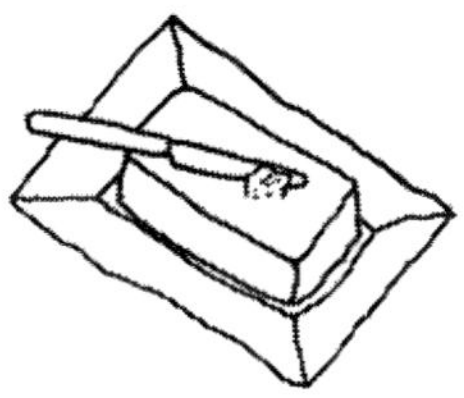

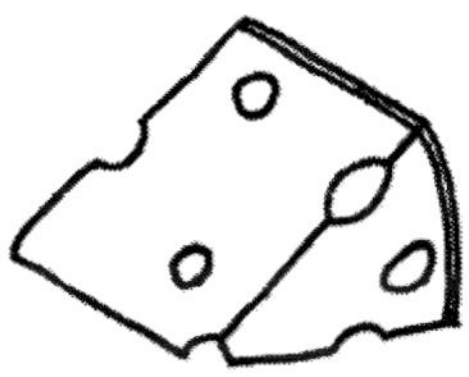

le	le	le	la	le
pain	**beurre**	**fromage**	**confiture**	**lait**

Mon nom ....

J'ai faim.

f	z	j	l	e	t	c
r	d	s	a	t	a	o
o	u	b	i	w	v	n
m	y	e	t	r	e	f
a	j	u	d	q	p	i
g	m	r	l	s	a	t
e	k	r	a	n	i	u
w	v	e	i	w	n	r
d	e	d	r	k	x	e

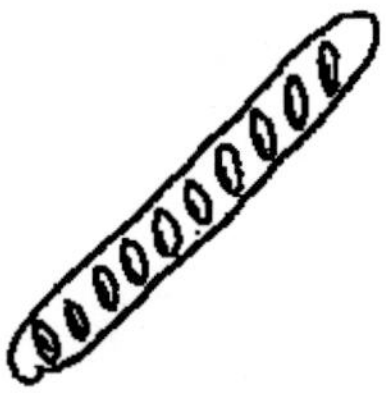

le **pain**

le ....

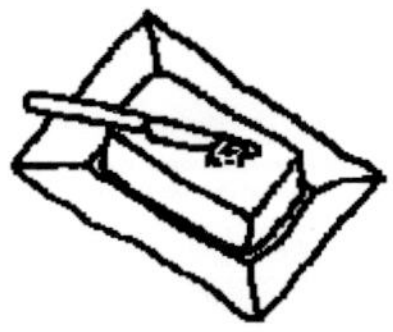

le **beurre**

le ....

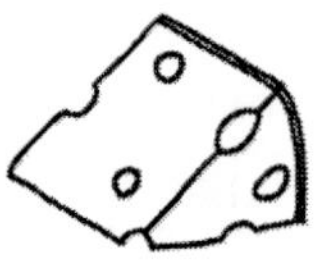

le **fromage**

le ....

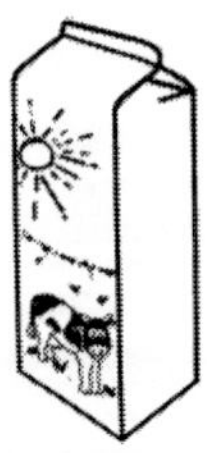

le **lait**

le ....

la **confiture**

la ....

Mon nom ....

Compte, calcule et écris

1	2	3	4	5	6	7	8	9	10
un	deux	trois	quatre	cinq	six	sept	huit	neuf	dix

 **–** 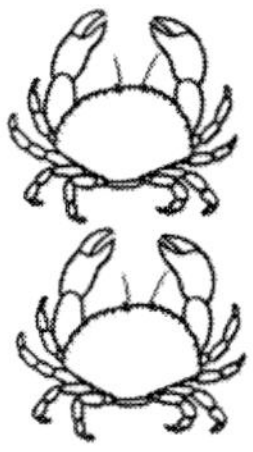 **=** 

....

 **–**  **=** 

....

 **–** 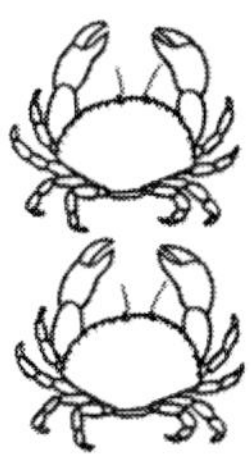 **=** 

....

 **–** 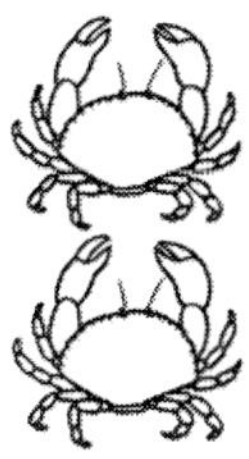 **=** 

....

 **–**  **=** 

....

Page 15 'J'ai faim. (ii)' – I'm hungry.

Page 15 :1

Colour correctly

Listen to the CD

Colorie la bonne image – Colour the correct picture

This is a listening and shape exercise.

Listen to the CD and write the colour the food in its correct shape. Make sure the children recognise all the shapes in English before playing the CD.

CD Script

Colorie les frites dans le cercle.
Colour the chips in the circle.
Colorie les pâtes dans le rectangle.
Colour the pasta in the rectangle.
Colorie l'oeuf dans l'ovale.
Colour the egg in the oval.
Colorie le miel dans le carré.
Colour the honey in the square.

Page 15 :2

Word search

J'ai faim – I'm hungry.

Look at the picture and write the correct French word on the dotted line beside each food item.

For those who like colouring, the whole page can be coloured.

For those who don't like colouring, they can colour code the picture next to the dotted line and its place in the picture.

Page 15 :3

Food sources in French

Écris le bon numéro – Write the correct number

Look at each item of food in the bottom half of the page.
Check the children know where the food comes from.
See if they can add some other examples.

All the children need to do is write the correct number linking the source (top half of the page) with its product (bottom half of the page).

If time, at the end of the lesson, the teacher could call out a food in French and the children can reply in ENGLISH where the food comes from. eg le pain – WHEAT l'œuf - HEN

The Felt Game

Revision of colours

The Felt Game Children stand in a circle

Put 10 coloured felt squares neatly in the centre of the circle.

One child stands in the middle of the circle.

Whilst singing '**Frère Jacques**' the other children walk **SLOWLY** round in a circle (holding hands) but facing outwards and the child in the middle takes one felt square and sits on it so it is hidden.
On the last word of the song (dong) the children in the circle jump round facing inwards and sit down.

They have to guess which colour the child in the middle is hiding.

Mon nom ....

Colorie la bonne image

Mon nom ....

J'ai faim.

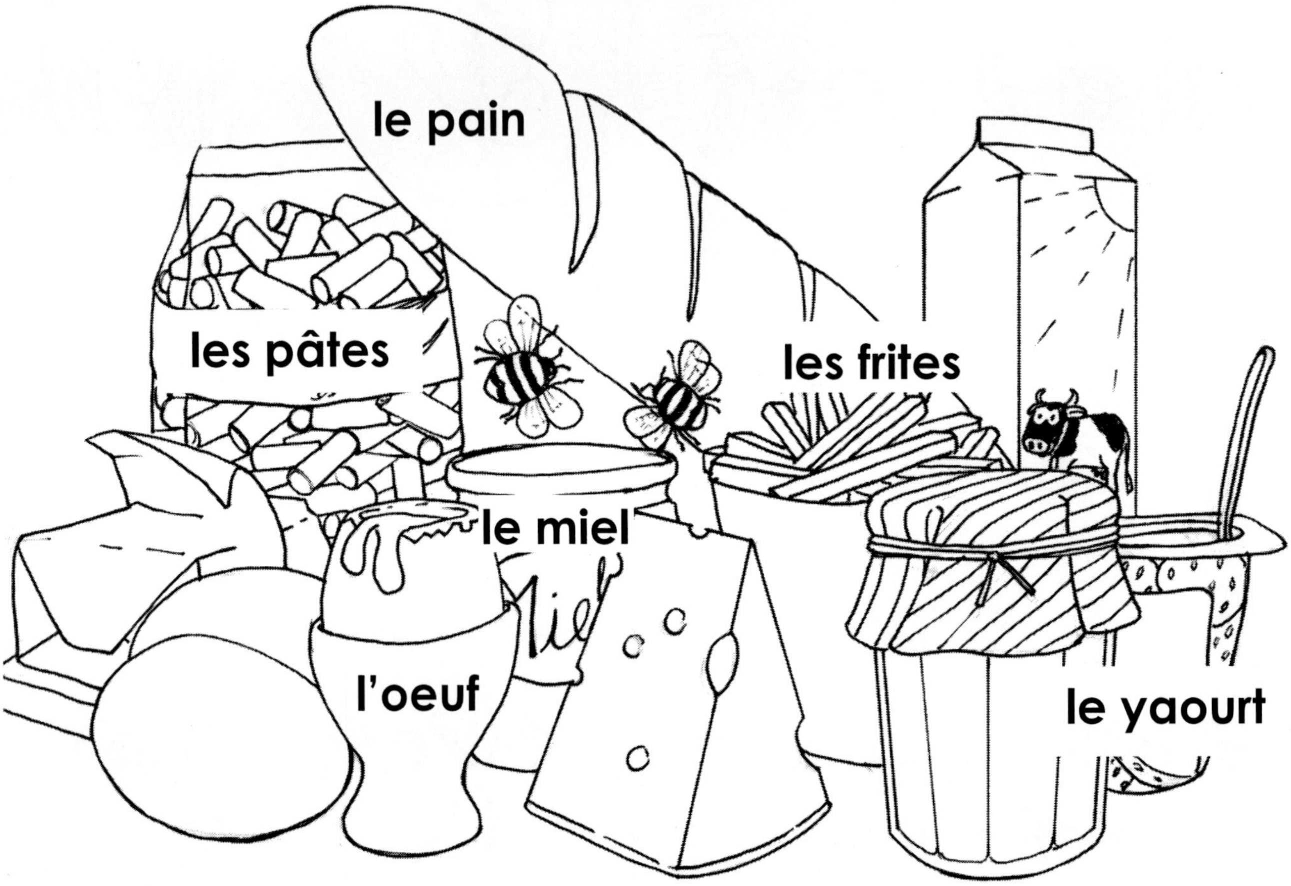

le

yaourt

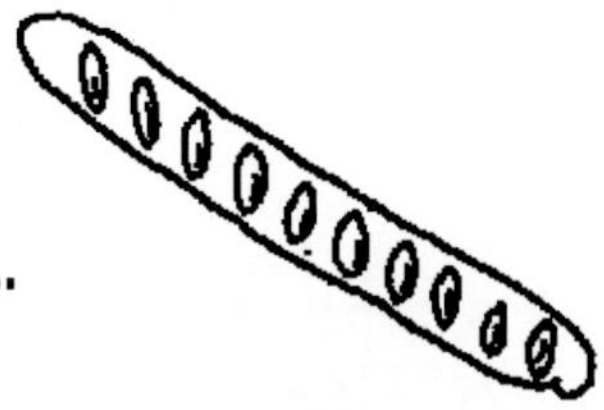

le

....

les

....

le

....

les

....

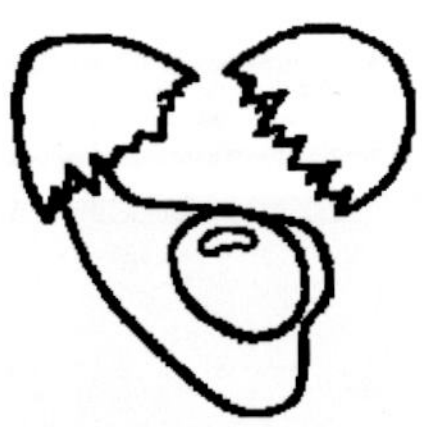

l'

....

Mon nom ....

Écris le bon numéro

1

2

3

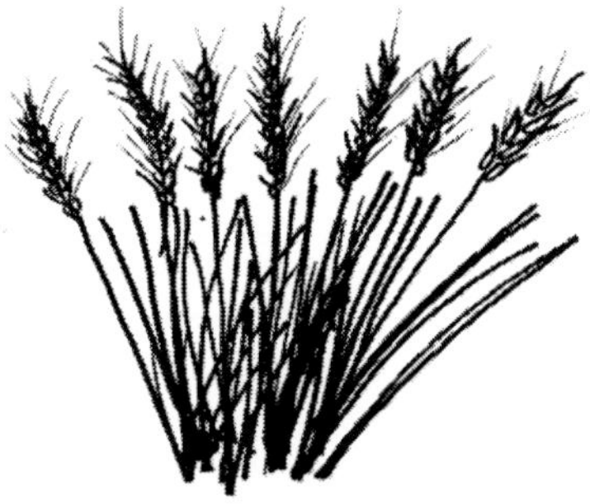

4

5

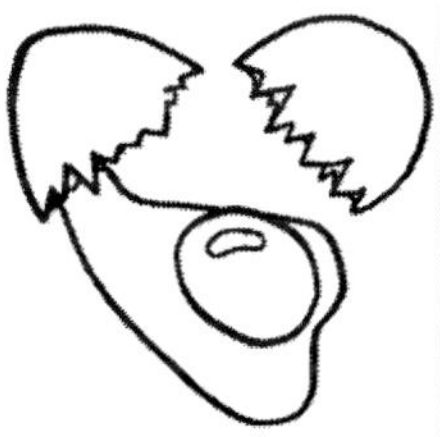

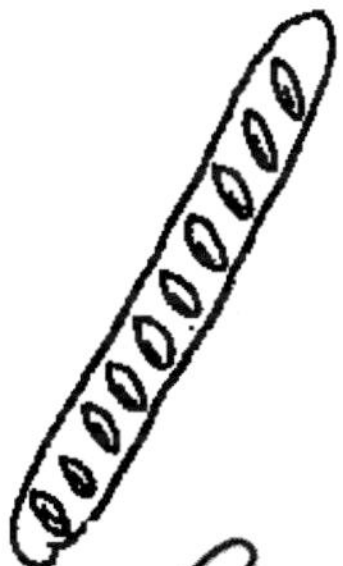

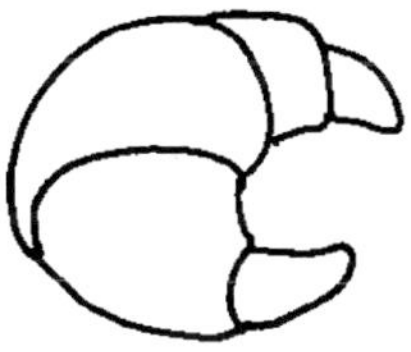

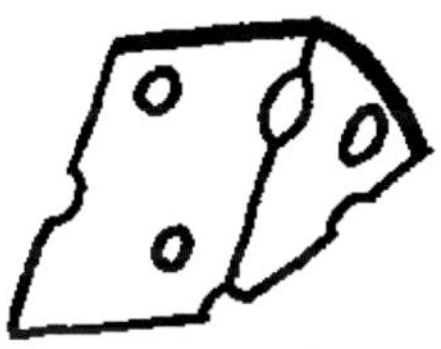

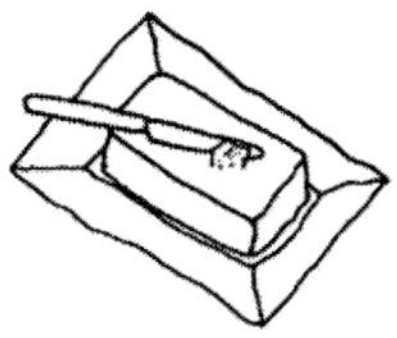

Page 16 'Comment tu t'appelles?' – What's your name?

Page 16 :1

Comment tu t'appelles?

Listen to the CD

Comment tu t'appelles? – What's your name?

Here is the beginning of spoken French.
Introduce the question "Comment tu t'appelles?"
Ask a few children their name and get them to reply "Je m'appelle..."

Then listen to the CD and look at the picture.

CD Script

Comment tu t'appelles? Je m'appelle Sophie.
Comment tu t'appelles? Je m'appelle Hubert.
Comment tu t'appelles? Je m'appelle Patrice.
Comment tu t'appelles? Je m'appelle Emilie.
Comment tu t'appelles? Je m'appelle Gilbert.

The children can colour in the picture listening to track 17 of the **CD**.
This will introduce them to the traditional French song:
"Savez-vous planter les choux?"

Page 16 :2

Craft in French

Making place names

Each child chooses a place name and writes his/her name as colourfully as possible on the dotted line and colours the picture.

Cut out the place name and stick/sellotape® the flap at the bottom to make a standing pyramid shape.

Practise asking the children "Comment tu t'appelles?"

Page 16 :3

Spot the difference

Trouve les 10 différences – Spot the difference

1. The rope on the climbing frame.
2. The white lines on the playground
3. The mouse's tail
4. The hedgehog's nose
5. The climbing frame step
6. The octopus' eye
7. The hedgehog's hand
8. The giraffe's ear
9. The elephant's toes
10. The giraffe's leg.

Pages 3 & 17

Traditional French Songs

Frère Jacques and **Savez-vous planter les choux?**

These two traditional French songs should be learnt by heart.

Once the class is confident in singing them, they could do a short performance to the rest of the school in assembly time.

Excellent practice for building up confidence in speaking a foreign language.

Mon nom ....

Comment tu t'appelles?

Comment tu t'appelles?

Je m'appelle

Je m'appelle

Mon nom ....

Trouve les 10 différences

Savez-vous planter les choux?

Savez-vous planter les choux?
À la mode, à la mode
Savez-vous planter les choux?
À la mode de chez nous

On les plante avec la main
À la mode, à la mode
On les plante avec la main
À la mode de chez nous

On les plante avec le pied ...

On les plante avec le nez ...

Mon nom ....

Savez-vous planter les choux?

Écris les nombres de l'histoire dans l'ordre.
Write the numbers of the story in order.

Page 18 **'un jeu'** – snakes and ladders

Page 18 :1

Dans sa maison

Listen to the CD

Dans sa maison un renard – In his house, a fox

This is a song/chant with actions.

1. In his house, a fox
Pretend to go round (with your hands) the shape of an enormous square in the air.
2. Looks out of his window
Make circles with thumb and index finger and hold them up to your eyes
3. and sees a rabbit coming by
With your hands pretend to be clawing a hole (like a dog) in the air
4. knocking at the door
Pretend to be knocking at the door
5. Help me help me the rabbit says
Hold both arms high in the air (twice) as if being told to put your hands up!
6. or else the hunter will kill me
Pretend to shoot
7. Rabbit, rabbit come inside
Pretend to beckon someone to you (As is saying "Come over here")
8. and shake me by the hand
Hold both hands together as if shaking them in a welcome

Page 18 :2

Measuringi n French

Mesure les animaux – Measure the animals

Each child needs a ruler.
The height or width of each animal needs to be measured. To make the exercise easier, an arrow has been included to help the children measure accurately.

When the measurement (to the nearest whole centimetre) has been found the number has to be written in full on the dotted line.

Answers

a. six b. dix c. cinq d. huit e. neuf

Page 18 :3

Observe and count in French

un jeu – a game

This is a game of snakes and ladders.
You go up the ladders and down the snakes.

This game can either be played with a dice in class or using the pre-set numbers below. (The advantage of playing the game with pre-set numbers is that the game is completed in six goes.

Pre-set numbers

trois quatre un deux deux cinq

deux trois quatre trois cinq deux

Skoldo French Songs

Un oiseau, deux oiseaux	**Page 7**
Cinq petits vers	**Page 10**
Où est le grand lion?	**Page 13**

Mon nom ....

Dans sa maison un renard

la fenêtre

le renard

1. Dans une **maison** un **renard**
2. regardait par la **fenêtre**
3. un **lapin** venir au loin
4. frapper à **la porte**
5. Aide-moi, aide-moi le lapin dit
6. ou **le chasseur** me tuera
7. lapin lapin entre et viens
8. **me serrer la main**

la maison

la porte

le lapin

le chasseur

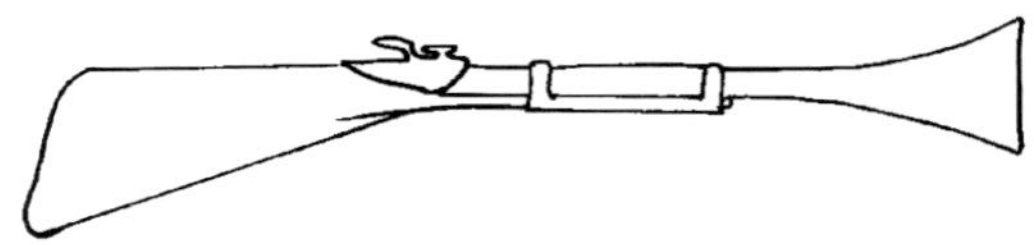

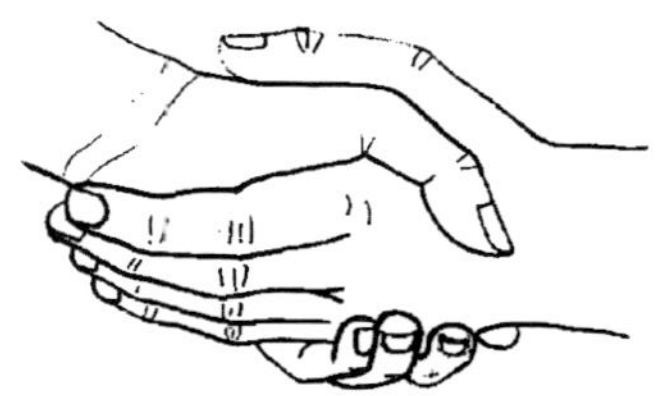
me serrer la main

Mon nom ....

Mesure les animaux

5 cinq 6 six 8 huit 9 neuf 10 dix

a Je mesure ....centimètres.

b Je mesure ....centimètres.

c Je mesure ....centimètres.

d Je mesure ....centimètres.

e Je mesure ....centimètres.

Tear off this corner
to make a counter

un jeu

Page 19 'les révisions' – revision

Page 19 :1

Count & colour

Listen to the CD

Écoute et colorie – Listen and colour

This is a whole class activity and listening exercise.

Go over all 10 colours (use the felts for their visual effects)

Revise numbers 1 – 10 (try and vary the counting by counting backwards, counting the even **(pair)** numbers and then the odd **(impair)** numbers.)

CD Script

Circle the words in their correct colours and then colour the pictures.

Colorie le pantalon en gris.	Colour the trousers grey.
Colorie le pull en bleu.	Colour the jumper blue.
Colorie les chaussures en marron.	Colour the shoes brown.
Colorie la chemise en jaune.	Colour the shirt yellow.
Colorie les chaussettes en orange.	Colour the socks orange.
Colorie le jean en rouge.	Colour the jeans red.
Colorie le tee-shirt en vert.	Colour the tee-shirt green.
Colorie la jupe en rose.	Colour the skirt pink.
Colorie la robe en violet.	Colour the dress purple.
Colorie les baskets en noir.	Colour the trainers black.

Page 19 :2

Observe and count in French

loto– bingo

NB When photocopying make sure the teacher has a copy so he/she can tick off the food and colours as a reference.

This is a revision exercise for food and colours.
So everyone can play, even the poor readers, all the colours are in symbol and written form (no reading is required).

1st game: Ask the children to colour in 5 foods.
Start reading out the foods.
The children cross out the foods they have coloured in.

The winner is the first child to cross out all 5 pictures.
This game can be played four times (2 x colours 2 x foods).

Page 19 :3

Colour the shirts

Colorie les chemises – Colour the shirts

This is an activity for everyone.

1. Look at the shirts and their patterns.
2. Find the small sample of each of the shirt's pattern and colour that shirt in the correct colour.

Felt game

As-tu le bleu?

As-tu le bleu? Have you got the blue? Children sit in a circle

Take ten coloured felt squares and whilst singing '**Frère Jacques**' get the children to pass the felts round in a circle.
On the last word of the song (dong) the children with the felt squares sit on them (the others pretend to do the same).
Children take it in turns to ask each other "As-tu le (whatever colour)?" until the correct child has been asked.
Keep going until all the colours have been discovered.

Mon nom ....

Écoute et colorie

1	2	3	4	5
bleu	rouge	rose	jaune	violet
6	7	8	9	10
vert	marron	orange	gris	noir

1 	2 	3 	4 	5 
6 	7 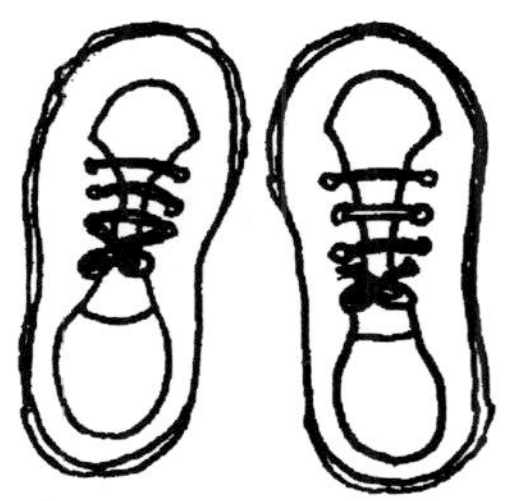	8 	9 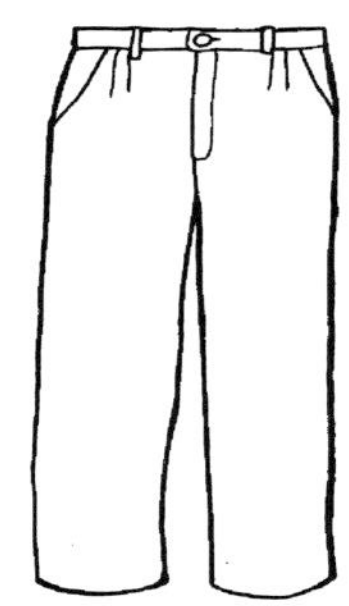	10 

Mon nom ....

loto

le pain | le fromage | la confiture | les pâtes | les frites | le yoourt | le lait | le beurre | l' oeuf | le miel

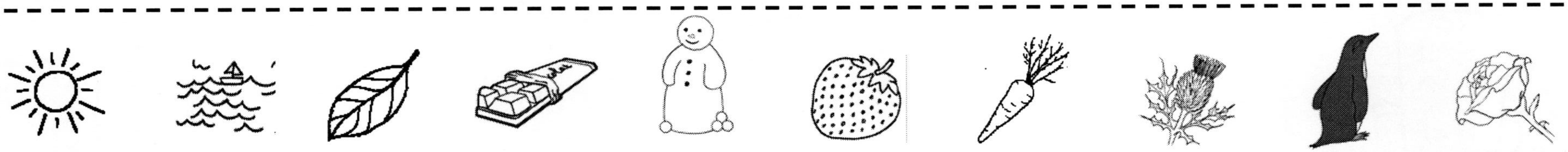

jaune | bleu | vert | marron | blanc | rouge | orange | violet | noir | rose

le pain | le fromage | la confiture | les pâtes | les frites | le yoourt | le lait | le beurre | l' oeuf | le miel

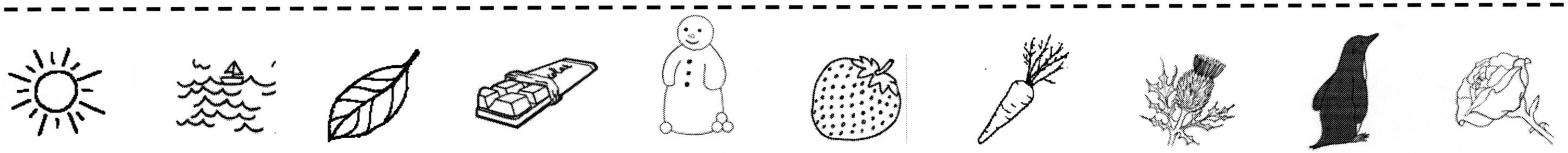

jaune | bleu | vert | marron | blanc | rouge | orange | violet | noir | rose

Mon nom ....

Colorie les chemises

 **rouge**

 **marron**

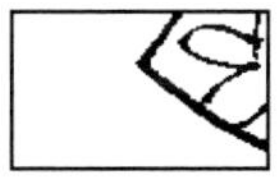 **vert**

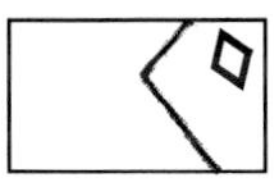 **bleu**

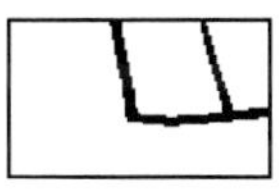 **rose**

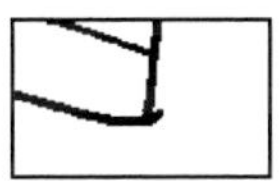 **violet**

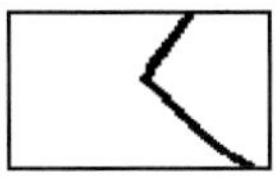 **jaune**

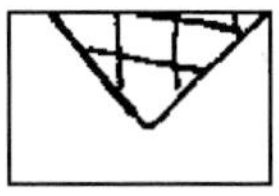 **orange**

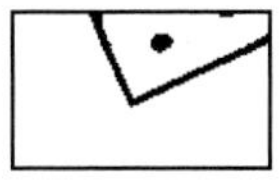 **gris**

Je vois deux chaussettes

Je vois deux chaussettes,
Je vois un jean bleu,
Je vois une jupe et un pull-over
Je vois deux chaussettes,
Je vois un jean bleu,
Je vois une jupe et un nounours

20:1 (Track 59 Karaoke version)

et le nounours!

Fold along this line

Page 21 'les animaux (i)' - animals

Page 21 :1

Beware of the cauliflowers!

Listen to the CD

Attention aux choux-fleurs! – Beware of the cauliflowers!

This is a dice game.
Fold the paper along the dotted line. One side for each game.

The teacher throws a dice and reads out the number followed by the French for the picture in the box.

The aim of the game is to colour in (very quickly) all five pictures before three 6s (the cauliflowers) have been thrown.

CD Script (If you do not wish to play with a dice)

Game 1: You lose

trois le lapin	**deux le chien**	**cinq le hamster**	**un le chat**
trois le lapin	**six le chou-fleur**	**cinq le hamster**	**six le chou-fleur**
un le chat	**deux le chien**	**trois le lapin**	**six le chou-fleur**

Game 2: You win

un le chat	**quatre le poisson**	**six le chou-fleur**	**un le chat**
trois le lapin	**six le chou-fleur**	**deux le chien**	**quatre le poisson**
deux le chien	**trois le lapin**	**trois le lapin**	**cinq le hamster**

Page 21 :2

Word recognition in French

Trouve l'intrus – Find the odd one out

This exercise is for the children who find writing easy.

All they have to do is circle the odd picture in each line and then write its French name on the dotted line.

All worksheets marked **:2** should be completed neatly and accurately.

Page 21 :3

Word recognition in French

Entoure le bon mot – Circle the correct word

This exercise is ideal for early readers and does not involve writing.

Go over the vocabulary of the animals with the class and remind them that the H in hamster is not pronounced.

The correct words for each picture need to be circled.

The picture or words can be coloured in. (Not all children like colouring)

Game

Animal Pelmanism

Pelmanism Children sit in a circle

Tear up small pieces of paper (one piece for each child)
Write, in French, the name of an animal on each piece of paper.
At this stage the children only know 5 animals.

Hand out a piece of paper to each child.
Choose one child to stand in the middle of the circle.
He makes his animal noise and then calls out a child's name.
That child makes his animal noise.
If they are the same they score a point and sit together.
Another child goes into the centre and makes his noise etc etc

Mon nom ....

Attention aux choux-fleurs!

Mon nom ....

Trouve l'intrus

 le **chien**  le **chat**  le **lapin**  le **hamster**  le **poisson**

le ....

le ....

le ....

le ....

le ....

Mon nom ....

Entoure le bon mot

le **hamster**	le **chien**	le **chat**	le **poisson**	le **lapin**

Page 22 'les animaux (ii)' - animals

Page 22 :1

How many?

Listen to the CD

Combien d'animaux y a-t-il? – How many animals are there?

This is a pure listening exercise.

Revise numbers 1 – 10
Explain that **Il y a** means There is/There are
Go over all the sentences orally with the children.
Revise or introduce the words la vache, le cochon, le mouton, le nuage and l'escargot.

Listen to the CD and colour in the correct number of pictures.

CD Script

Il y a huit vaches.	**une deux trois quatre cinq six sept huit**
Il y a sept cochons.	**un deux trois quatre cinq six sept**
Il y a neuf moutons.	**un deux trois quatre cinq six sept huit neuf**
Il y a deux nuages.	**un deux**
Il y a un escargot.	**un**

Page 22 :2

Maths in French

Compte, calcule et écris – Count, add and write.

This exercise is ideal for children who find writing and maths easy.

All they have to do is look up the number which goes with each picture, add the numbers together and write the new number in the answer section, drawing its picture in the box.

All worksheets marked **:2** should be completed neatly and accurately.

Page 22 :3

Word search in French

les animaux – animals

This wordsearch can be used for able writers and early learners.

1. The able writers need to copy the words on the dotted lines.
2. The less fluent writers need only find the words in the wordsearch.

For those who like colouring, each letter (of the hidden word) can be coloured. For those who don't like colouring, they can design patterns in the boxes where the letters are found.

Animal Pelmanism

Pelmanism Children sit in a circle

Tear up small pieces of paper (one piece for each child)
Write, in French, the name of an animal on each piece of paper.
At this stage in their learning they know 10 animals.

Hand out one piece of paper to each child.
Choose one child to stand in the middle of the circle.
He makes his animal noise and then calls out a child's name.
That child makes his animal noise. If they are the same they score a point and sit together. Each child has two goes.
Another child goes into the centre and makes his noise etc etc

Mon nom ....

Combien d'animaux y a-t-il?

un(e)	deux	trois	quatre	cinq	six	sept	huit	neuf	dix
1	2	3	4	5	6	7	8	9	10

Il y a huit vaches.

une deux trois quatre cinq six sept huit

Il y a sept cochons.

un deux trois quatre cinq six sept

Il y a neuf moutons.

un deux trois quatre cinq six sept huit neuf

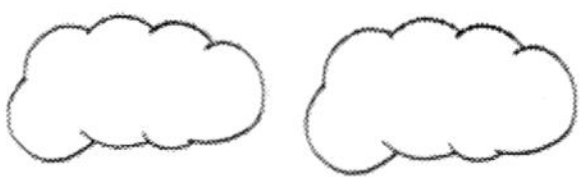

Il y a deux nuages.

un deux

Il y a un escargot.

un

Mon nom ....

Compte, calcule et écris

un	deux	trois	quatre	cinq	six	sept	huit	neuf	dix

_ _ _ _ + _ _ _ _ _ _ = _ _ _ _

_ _ _ + _ _ = _ _ _ _

_ _ _ _ _ + _ _ _ _ = _ _ _ _

_ _ _ _ + _ _ _ _ _ = _ _ _

_ _ _ _ + _ _ _ _ _ _ = _ _ _

Mon nom ....

les animaux

f	z	c	l	e	t	c
m	d	h	a	p	j	o
o	g	e	s	o	f	c
u	p	v	m	u	e	h
t	j	a	d	l	p	o
o	m	l	x	e	a	n
n	k	r	a	n	g	u
w	v	a	c	h	e	x
d	e	d	r	k	b	e

le **mouton**

le ....

le **cheval**

le ....

la **vache**

la ....

la **poule**

la ....

le **cochon**

le ....

Toc! Toc! Toc!

Toc! Toc! Toc!
Qui est là, à la porte?
Ouaf! ouaf! ouaf!
Qui est là?
C'est le chien.

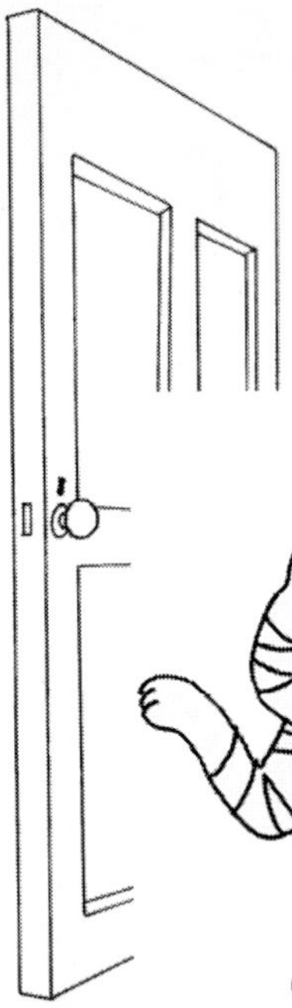

Toc! Toc! Toc!
Qui est là, à la porte?
Miaou! miaou! miaou!
Qui est là?
C'est le chat.

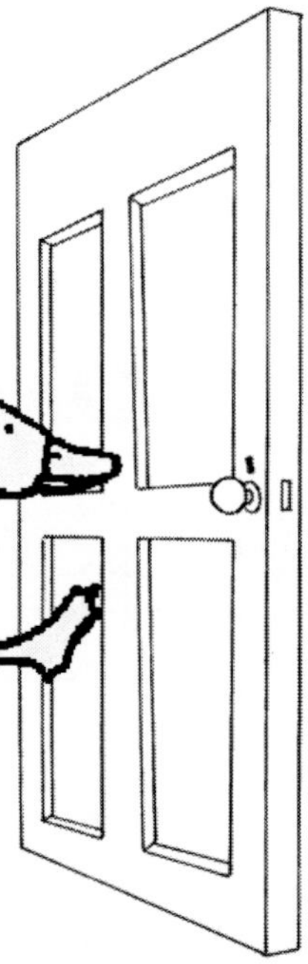

Toc! Toc! Toc!
Qui est là, à la porte?
Coin! coin! coin!
Qui est là?
C'est le canard.

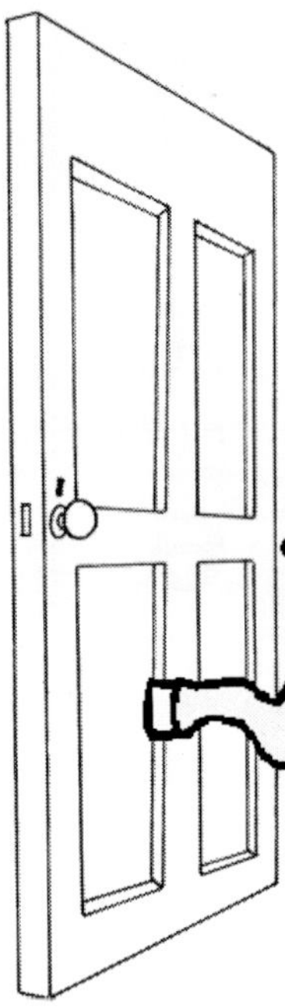

Toc! Toc! Toc!
Qui est là, à la porte?
Meuh! meuh! meuh!
Qui est là?
C'est la vache.

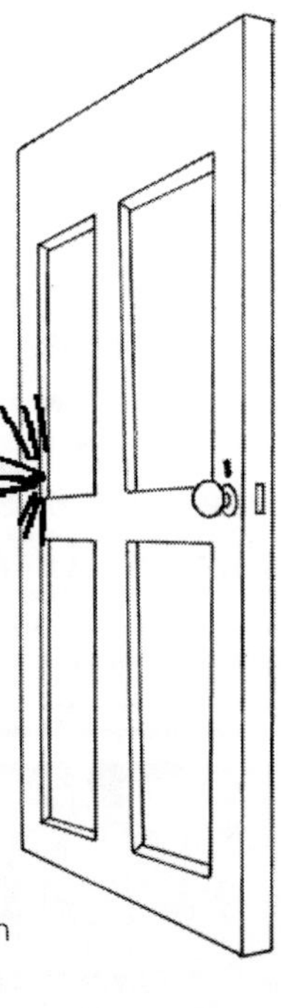

Toc! Toc! Toc!
Qui est là, à la porte?
Cui! cui! cui!
Qui est là?
C'est l'oiseau.

Toc!
Toc! Toc!

....

C'est
le chien

un

C'est
le chat

deux

C'est
le canard

trois

C'est
la vache

quatre

C'est
l'oiseau

cinq

Page 24 'les fruits' - fruit

Page 24 :1

Sound lotto

Listen to the CD

loto – Lotto

This is a pure listening exercise.

Go over all the vocabulary with the children.
Make sure the children know which animal makes what noise.
Each child circles one of the four boxes (each box contains six animals)

Listen to the CD and cross out an animal in the box when you hear the sound. The winner is the first child to cross out all six animals.

CD Script

(The CD has two games pre-recorded. To cover all four games play the CD track twice.)

le lion	**la vache**	**le chien**	**le chat**	**le mouton**
le cochon	**le cheval**	**l'oiseau**	**la poule**	**le loup**
le chat	**l'oiseau**	**la vache**	**le loup**	**le chien**
le cochon	**le mouton**	**le cheval**	**le lion**	**la poule**

Page 24 :2

Co-ordinates in French

Dessine dans les carrés – Draw in the squares

This exercise is fine for the children who find writing easy and understand the concept of co-ordinates.

All worksheets marked **:2** should be completed neatly and accurately.

Page 24 :3

Letter recognition in French

Cherche et colorie les lettres – Look for and colour the letters

This exercise is aimed at helping children recognize letters and spelling.

Each picture is labelled in French.
Find and circle or colour all the letters that make up the French word for each picture.

Skoldo Songs and game

Toc! Toc! Toc! (page 23) and Cinq petits vers (page 10)

See if they can make up actions to go with the song Toc! Toc! Toc!

Divide the class into two. One half performs Toc! Toc! Toc! to the other and then the other half performs Cinq petits vers.

GAME "Cinq petits vers" Everyone sits in a circle and sings the first verse.

Whilst singing the second verse, one child goes slowly round the outside of the circle patting the head of every child in time to each word in the song (**Un** PAT **deux** PAT **trois** PAT **quatre** PAT **blank** that child is out and sits in the middle. You go on singing the song and everytime the **blank** is shown/sung that child is out. At the end of the song, all the children left in the circle have been spared being eaten by the blackbird.

Those in the middle have been eaten!

Mon nom ....

loto

le lion | la vache | le chien | le chat | le mouton | le cochon | le cheval | l'oiseau | la poule | le loup

Mon nom ....

Dessine dans les carrés

	a	b	c
1			
2			
3			

une banane  3 b

....

une pomme  1 a

....

une poire  3 c

....

une fraise  2 b

....

un citron 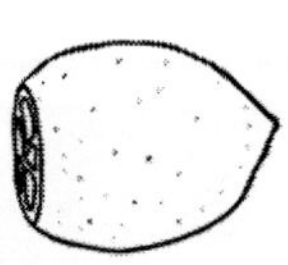 1 c

....

Mon nom ....

Cherche et colorie les lettres

  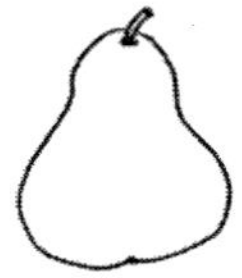  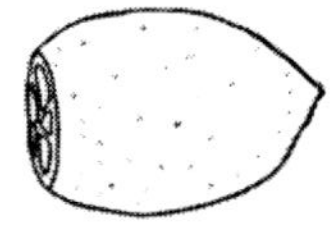

la **banane** la **pomme** la **poire** la **fraise** le **citron**

 j b v a k d n s r a p n m e i

 p n v o u d m s o m j r e i s

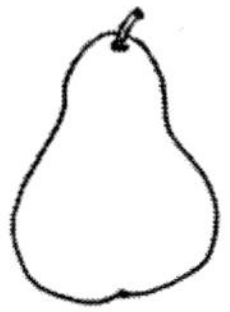 z j c v p a g o s d i k r w t e

 g c m f o k r q a i z n s x e

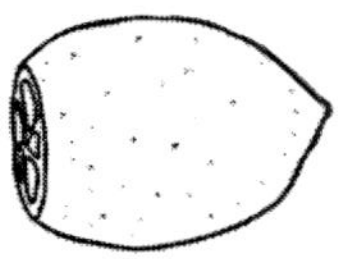 c m i q v t u s r o w e n x

Page 25 'les légumes' - vegetables

Page 25 :1

Game

Listen to the CD

Un jeu – Game

This is a pure listening exercise.

Go over all the numbers and words with the children.
Revise the colours in French.
Listen to the CD and colour correctly each picture/number according to the instructions.
Colour each item very quickly to keep the lesson moving!!

CD Script

Colorie numéro cinq en gris.
Colorie numéro trois en bleu.
Colorie numéro deux en marron.
Colorie numéro cinq en violet.

Colorie numéro six en rouge.
Colorie numéro huit en vert.
Colorie numéro sept en orange.
Colorie numéro quatre en marron.

Colorie la banane en jaune.
Colorie la pomme en vert.
Colorie la fraise en rouge.
Colorie l'orange en orange.

Colorie la chemise en jaune.
Colorie la jupe en rose.
Colorie le pull en violet.
Colorie le jean en bleu.

Page 25 :2

Word recognitioni n French

Trouve l'intrus – Find the odd one out

This exercise is for the children who find writing easy.

All they have to do is circle the odd picture in each line and then write its French name on the dotted line.

All worksheets marked **:2** should be completed neatly and accurately.

Page 25 :3

Observation and drawing

Dessine les légumes – Draw the vegetables

1. Go over all the vocabulary.
2. Check the children know which vegetables grow above and which grow below the ground.

Those who like colouring, can colour the whole picture.
Those who don't like colouring, can colour the vegetables only.

Skoldo

Vegetable Chant

The vegetable chant + actions

(See pictures on 25:3 for illustrated pictures)

1. Chant **une car otte** and on each syllable tap the head (x 3)
2. Chant **une tom ate** and on each syllable click fingers (x 3)
3. Chant **un oig non** and on each syllable clap hands (x 3)
4. Chant **une pomme d' terre** and on each syllable pat the desk with palms of hands (x 3) (**de terre** can be said as one syllable)
5. As you chant **et un chou-fleur** make a large round circular shape in the air with both hands.

Mon nom ....

un jeu

Listen to the CD and colour in the picture or number when you hear its French name.

Mon nom ....

Trouve l'intrus

l'
onion

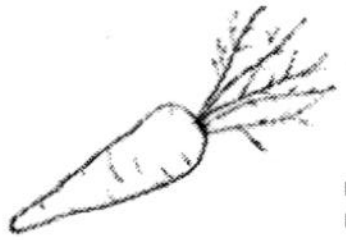
la
carotte

la
tomate

le
chou-fleur

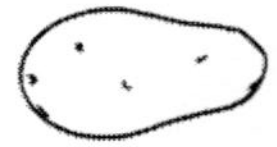
la
pomme de terre

le ....

la ....

la ....

la ....

l' ....

Mon nom ....

Dessine les légumes

la carotte	la tomate	l' oignon	la pomme de terre	le chou-fleur

Look at the picture above and draw the missing vegetables.

Page 26 'Quel âge as-tu?' – How old are you?

Page 26 :1

Quel âge as-tu?

Listen to the CD

Quel âge as-tu? – How old are you?

Here is some conversational French, introducing the question:
"Quel âge as-tu?"
Ask a few children how old they are and get them to reply "J'ai ... ans."
Remind them that, in English, you can answer **I'm six** but in French you have to add the **ans** (years) each time – **J'ai six ans.**

Listen to the CD and look at the picture.

CD Script

Quel âge as-tu Hubert? **J'ai cinq ans.**
Quel âge as-tu Patrice? **J'ai huit ans.**
Quel âge as-tu Emilie? **J'ai six ans.**
Quel âge as-tu Sophie? **J'ai quatre ans.**
Quel âge as-tu Gilbert? **J'ai sept ans.**

The children can colour in the picture listening to track 27 of the **CD**.
This will introduce them to the next Skoldo song "J'adore les glaces."

Page 26 :2

How old are you?

Quel âge as-tu?

Look at the six different children, their names and ages.

Ask the question "Quel âge as-tu?"

Write the correct number in French on the dotted line next to each child's picture. All the numbers are written at the top of the page.

Page 26 :3

Spot the difference

Trouve les 10 différences – Spot the difference

1. A missing puff of smoke
2. A missing railway wagon wheel
3. The mouse's tail
4. The elephant's leg
5. The mouse's ears
6. The octopus' picture
7. The train's engine funnel
8. The hedgehog's shoe lace
9. The giraffe's ear
10. The giraffe's legs

Revision

French songs and spoken French

Revision of French songs and spoken French

As this lesson is quite relaxing, you can end it with a free choice of French songs and revision of the conversation sheets.

French songs: Pages **3**, **7**, **10**, **13**, **17**, **20**, **23** and **27**

Conversation sheets: Pages **6**, **16** and **26**

Make sure all the appropriate sheets have been coloured in.

Mon nom ....

Quel âge as-tu?

Mon nom ....

Quel âge as-tu?

Look at ages of each child and write the number in full on the dotted line.

4	5	6
quatre	**cinq**	**six**

Lucas	Jade	Enzo

Emma	**Camille**	**Clément**

 **Lucas a** .... **ans.**

 **Jade a** .... **ans.**

 **Enzo a** .... **ans.**

 **Emma a** .... **ans.**

 **Camille a** .... **ans.**

 **Clément a** .... **ans.**

Mon nom ....

Trouve les 10 différences

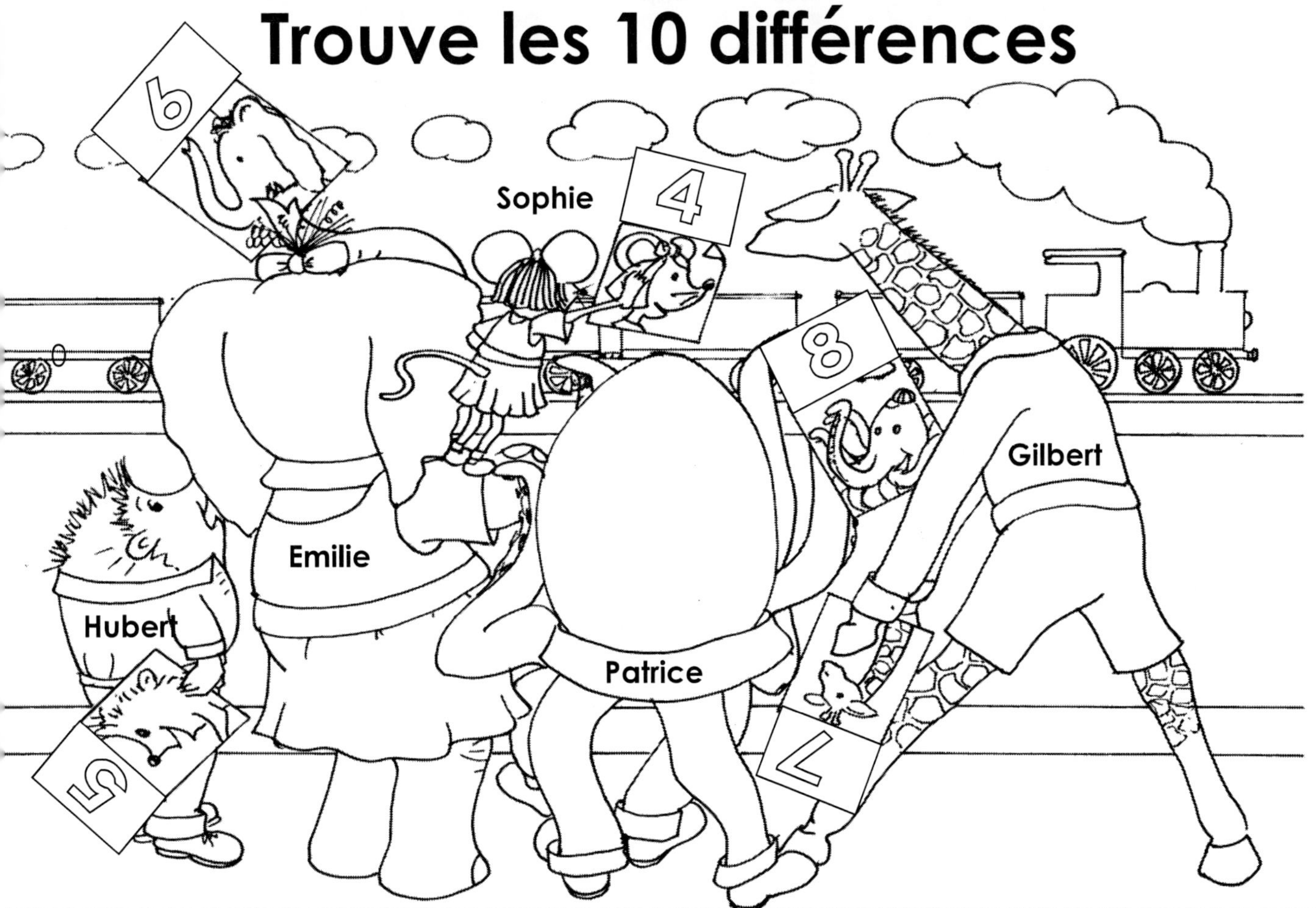

J’adore les glaces

J'adore les glaces, les glaces, les glaces
J'adore les glaces mmmmmm!

banane poire pomme citron ananas
J’adore les glaces
fraise orange

J'adore les fruits, les fruits, les fruits
J'adore les fruits mmmmmm!

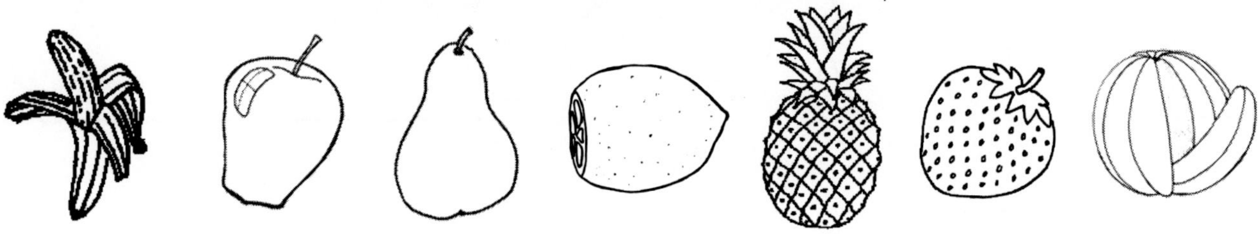

banane poire pomme citron ananas
J’adore les fruits
fraise orange

J'adore les bonbons, les bonbons, les bonbons
J'adore les bonbons mmmmmm!

banane poire pomme citron ananas
J’adore les bonbons
fraise orange

27:1 (Track 61 Karaoke version)

le
citron

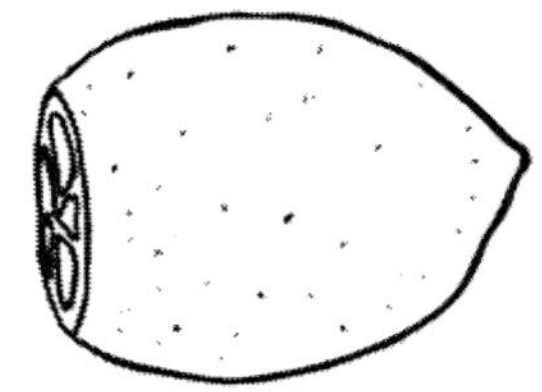

la
fraise

l'
orange

le
chocolat

Page 28 'les contes de fées' – Fairy Tales

Page 28 :1

les contes de fées

Listen to the CD

les contes de fées – Fairy Tales

Here are the titles of four famous fairy tales. Each story has a famous line.
Listen to the CD and work out which famous line goes with which story.

CD Script

les trois petits cochons	The three little pigs.
Boucle d'or et les trois ours	Goldilocks and the three bears
Blanche-neige et les sept nains	Snowwhite and the seven dwarfs.
le petit Chaperon rouge	Little red riding hood

Non, Non! Par le poil de mon menton! The three little pigs.
No, no by the hair of my chinny chin chin!

Quelqu'un a mangé ma soupe!! Goldilocks and the three bears
Someone's been eating my soup!

Miroir, miroir, dis-moi qui est la plus belle? Snow-white & the seven dwarfs.
Mirror Mirror on the wall, who's the fairest of them all?

Que vous avez de grands yeux ! Little red riding hood
What big eyes you have!

The children can colour in the picture listening to track 28

Page 28 :2

Maths in French

Compte, calcule et écris – Count, add and write.

This exercise is ideal for children who find writing and maths easy.

All they have to do is look up the number which goes with each picture, add the numbers together and write the new number in the answer section, drawing its picture in the box.

Worksheets marked **:2** should be completed neatly & accurately.

six (ladybird) **cinq** (hedgehog) **quatre** (mole) **huit** (hare) **sept** (cobweb)

Page 28 :3

How many wolves are there ?

Combien de loups y a-t-il? – How many wolves are there?

Practise counting up to 10 in French.

1. Count the number of wolves hidden in the bushes.
2. Colour the picture
3. Write the correct number at the bottom of the page.

Game

As-tu le bleu?

As-tu le bleu? Have you got the blue? Children sit in a circle

Take ten coloured felt squares.
Whilst singing '**Frère Jacques**' (See page 3) get the children to pass the felts round in a circle.
On the last word of the song (dong) the children with the felt squares sit on them (the others pretend to do the same).
Children take it in turns to ask each other "As-tu le (whatever colour)?" until the correct child has been asked.

Carry on until all the felt squares have been discovered.

les trois petits cochons

Boucle d'or et les trois ours

Blanche-neige
et les sept nains

le petit
Chaperon Rouge

Mon nom ....

Compte, calcule et écris

un	deux	trois	quatre	cinq	six	sept	huit	neuf	dix

_ _ _ _ – _ _ _ _ _ = _ _ _

_ _ _ – _ _ _ _ = _ _ _ _

_ _ _ – _ _ _ _ = _ _ _ _ _ _

_ _ _ _ – _ _ = _ _ _ _

_ _ _ – _ _ _ _ _ = _ _ _ _

Mon nom ....

Combien de loups y a-t-il?

1	2	3	4	5	6	7	8	9	10
un	deux	trois	quatre	cinq	six	sept	huit	neuf	dix

Il y a ___ ___ ___ ___ loups.

Page 29 'les révisions' – revision

Page 29 :1

Count & colour

Listen to the CD

Écoute et colorie – Listen and colour

This is a whole class activity and listening exercise.

1. Go over all 10 words and numbers 1 – 10.
2. Write the correct number in the correct box.

La vache est numéro quatre.	**Le chat est numéro neuf.**
Le cheval est numéro six.	**Le lapin est numéro dix.**
La poule est numéro trois.	**Le hamster est numéro sept.**
Le mouton est numéro deux.	**Le chien est numéro huit.**
Le cochon est numéro un.	**Le poisson est numéro cinq.**

Page 29 :2

Observe and count in French

loto– bingo

NB When photocopying make sure the teacher has a copy so he/she can tick off the pictures as a reference.

This is a revision exercise for animals, fruit, vegetables and numbers.
All the vocabulary is in picture form (no reading is required).
1st game: Ask the children to colour in 5 numbers.
Start reading out the numbers.
The children cross out the numbers they have coloured in.

The winner is the first child to cross out all 5 pictures.
This game can be played four times (2 x numbers 2 x vocab).

Page 29 :3

Observation in French

Colorie les paires – Colour the pairs

This is an activity for everyone.

1. Look at the shoes.
2. Find the small sample of each shoe and colour that shoe in its correct colour.

Fruit & Veg Miming

Fruit and vegetable miming

Children sit in a circle

Draw a picture of each fruit or vegetable, the children know in French, on each piece of paper.
There will be 10 pictures in all.
Fold the pieces up and ask a child to come and pick a piece of paper.

The child stands in the middle of the circle and proceeds to mime his picture.
He then calls out a child's name.
That child has to guess which fruit or veg is being acted out.
When it has been guessed he goes in the middle.

banana (peeling) apple (taking a bite) pear (pear shape with hands) lemon (bitter in mouth) strawberry (rub tummy!) onion (rub eyes) potato (dig) carrot (chop into slices) tomato (pick at tummy height) cauliflower (cut at ground level)

Mon nom ....

Écoute et colorie

1	2	3	4	5
le cochon	le mouton	la poule	la vache	le poisson
6	7	8	9	10
le cheval	le hamster	le chien	le chat	le lapin

Mon nom ....

loto

10	9	8	7	6	5	4	3	2	1
dix	neuf	huit	sept	six	cinq	quatre	trois	deux	un

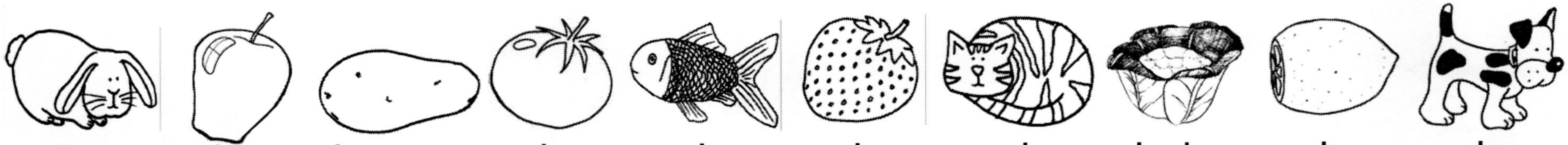

le lapin	la pomme	la pomme de terre	la tomate	le poisson	la fraise	le chat	le chou fleur	le citron	le chien

10	9	8	7	6	5	4	3	2	1
dix	neuf	huit	sept	six	cinq	quatre	trois	deux	un

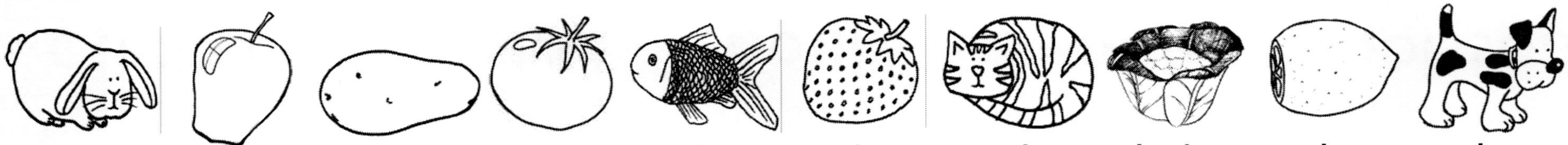

le lapin	la pomme	la pomme de terre	la tomate	le poisson	la fraise	le chat	le chou fleur	le citron	le chien

Mon nom ....

Colorie les paires

Colour the pair of shoes with the help of the small clue at the bottom of the page.

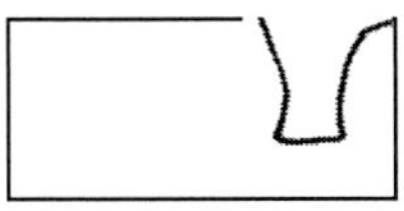 **rouge**

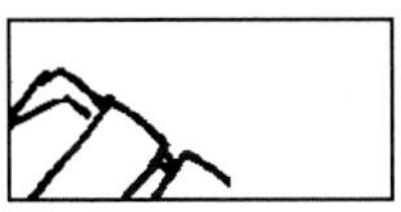 **marron**

 **bleu**

 **rose**

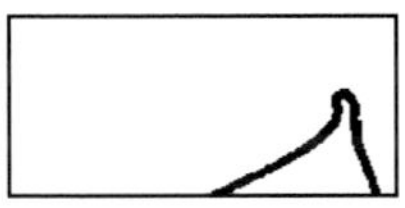 **jaune**

 **gris**

 **violet**

 **vert**

la soupe aux légumes

Oh! la soupe aux légumes
C'est délicieux
la soupe aux légumes

Oh! la soupe aux légumes
C'est délicieux
la soupe aux légumes

trois carottes

cinq pommes de terre

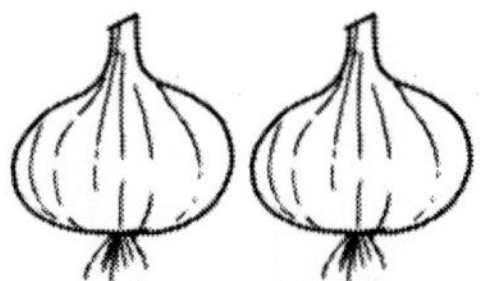

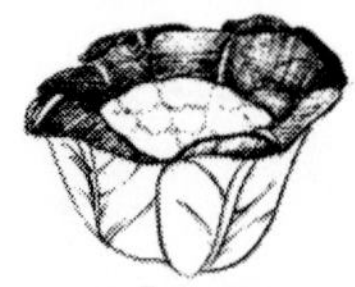

deux oignons

et un chou-fleur

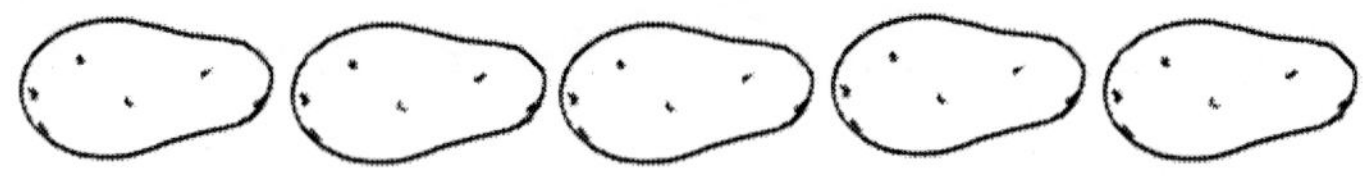

trois carottes

cinq pommes de terre

deux oignons

et quatre tomates

Oh! la soupe aux légumes
C'est délicieux
la soupe aux légumes

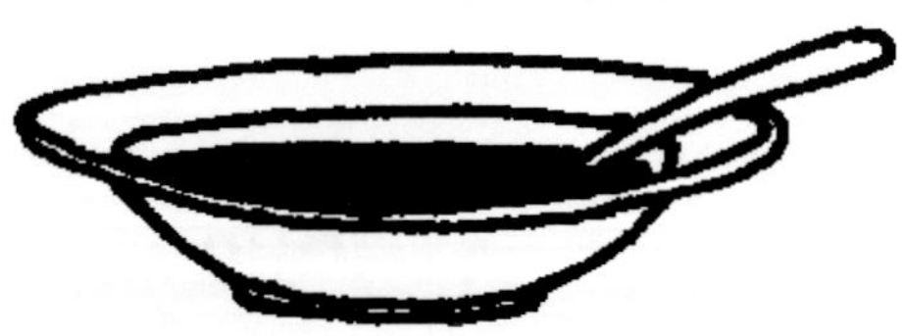

Oh! la soupe aux légumes
C'est délicieux
la soupe aux légumes

30:1 (Track 62 Karaoke version)

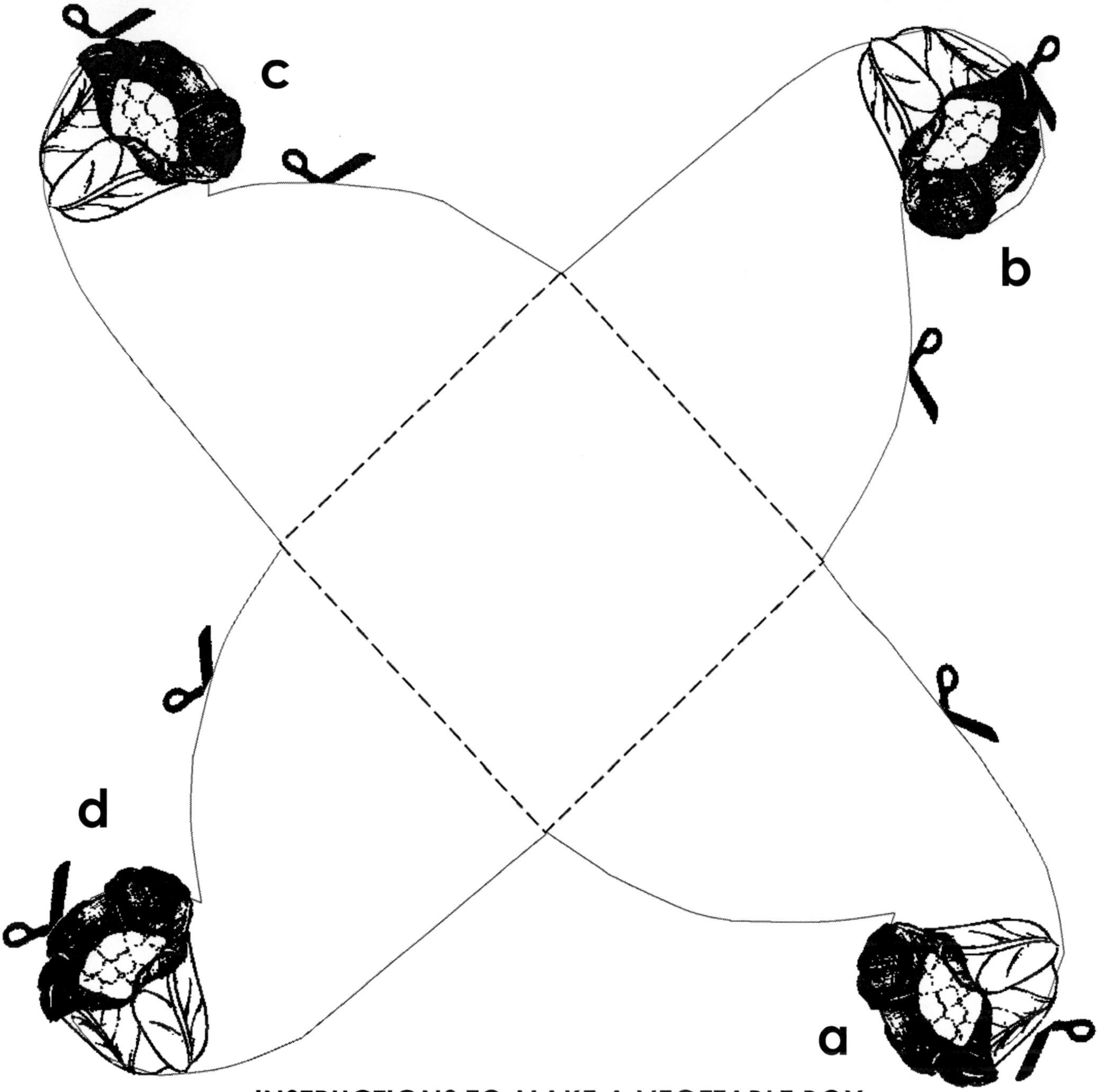

INSTRUCTIONS TO MAKE A VEGETABLE BOX

Write **a,b,c,d** behind each cauliflower when the box has been cut out.
Fold along the dotted lines with the cauliflowers facing outwards.
1. Hook **a** over **b**   2. Hook **d** over **a/b**   3. Hook **c** over **a/b/d**

Colour and cut out these vegetables and pop them into the 'SOUP BOX'

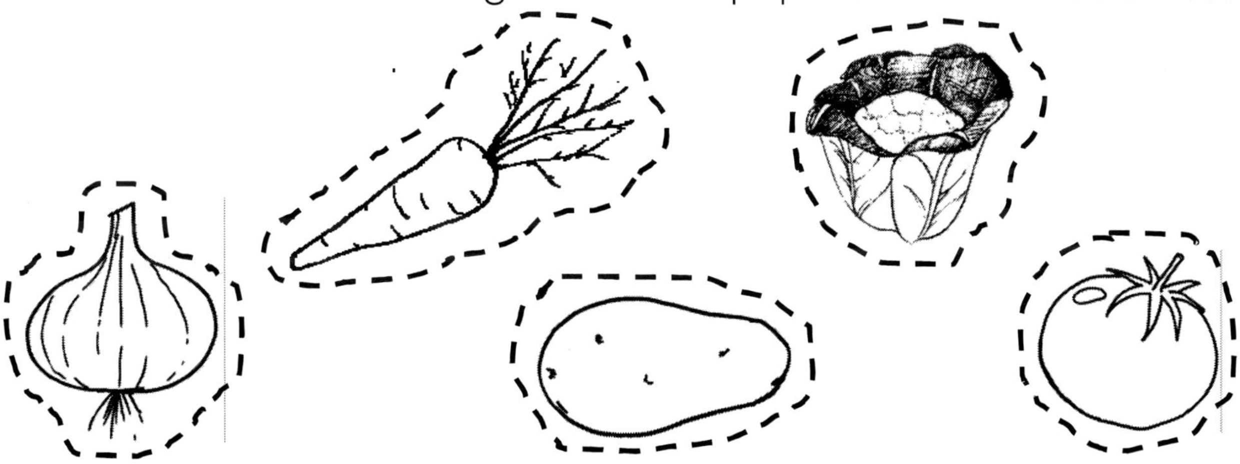

Page 31 'un jeu de dé' – a dice game

Page 31 :1

Dice Game Listen to the CD

Jeu de dé – Dice Game

This is a listening game similar to a Beetle Drive.

Revise numbers 1 – 6

1. Circle a face and listen to the CD.
2. As the numbers are read out, colour in that part of the face.
3. For eyes, cheeks and ears you need to hear the number read out twice.

CD Script (To play games three and four, you will need to re-start CD track 31)

Games 1 & 3 **2 4 3 4 2 1 3 1 4 5 3 6 2 1 2 5 4 6**

Games 2 & 4 **6 4 5 2 1 2 6 3 5 4 1 2 6 2 5 4 6 3**

Page 31 :2

Word recognition in French

Entoure le bon dessin – Circle the correct drawing

This exercise is for the children who find writing easy.

All they have to do is circle the picture which is associated with each part of the head. ie la tête – (circle the hat)

All worksheets marked **:2** should be completed neatly and accurately.

Page 31 :3

Observation and numbers

Entoure le bon numéro – Circle the correct number

Associate the small sections of the face with the main picture and circle the correct number.

There is no writing in this exercise.

For those who like colouring, the small sections can be coloured the same as the large picture.
For those who don't like colouring, they can design a shape in the background of each small picture and copy the shape in the correct square of the large picture.

Game Simon says

Jacques a dit Simon says

Jacques a dit touche la tête (touch your head)
Jacques a dit touche les yeux (touch your eyes)
Jacques a dit touche les oreilles (touch your ears)
Jacques a dit touche la bouche (touch your mouth)
Jacques a dit touche le nez (touch your nose)
Jacques a dit touche les cheveux (touch your hair)

Don't forget that when **you say Jacques a dit** ✓ you must obey the command
When you **do not say Jacques a dit** × you do not obey the command

Mon nom ....

un jeu de dé

Circle a head, then listen to the CD. As each number is read out, colour that part of the head only. If a number is read out and you have already coloured in that part of the face you must wait.

1	2	3	4	5	6
un	deux	trois	quatre	cinq	six

Mon nom ....

Écris le bon mot et entoure le bon dessin

la **tête**

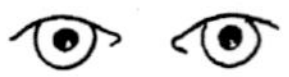
les **yeux**

la **bouche**

le **nez**

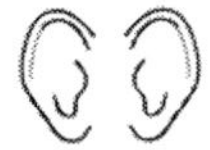
les **oreilles**

les **cheveux**

 la __ __ __ __

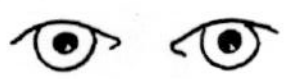 les __ __ __ __

 la __ __ __ __ __ __

 le __ __ __

 les __ __ __ __ __ __ __ __

 les __ __ __ __ __ __ __

Mon nom ....

Entoure le bon numéro

1 un **2** deux **3** trois **4** quatre **5** cinq

6 six **7** sept **8** huit **9** neuf **10** dix

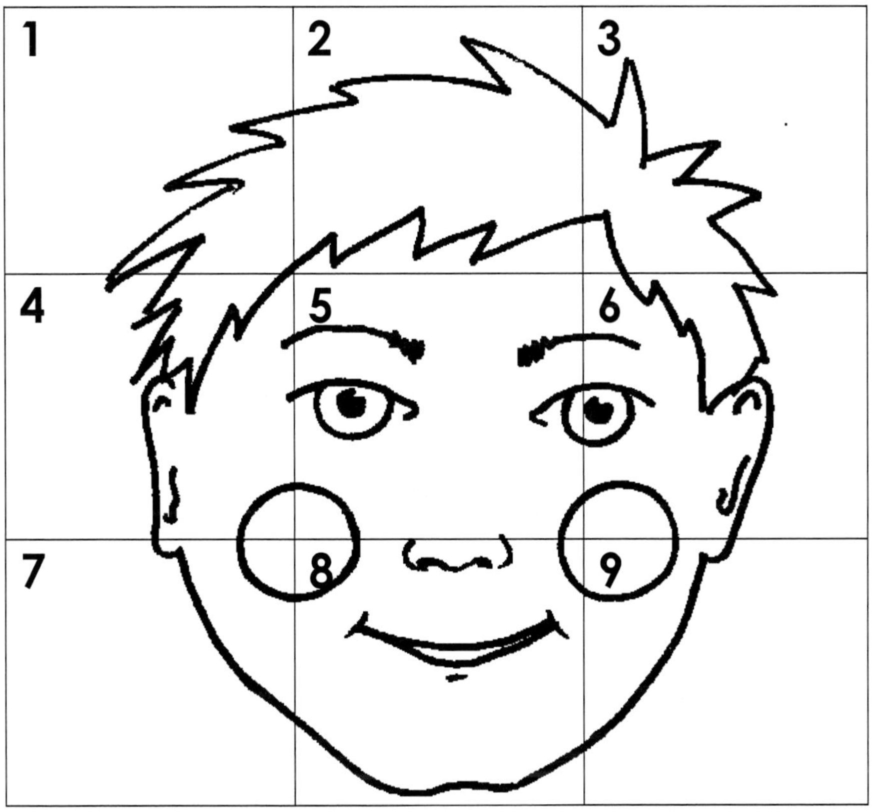

trois
sept
huit
cinq

huit
six
quatre
trois

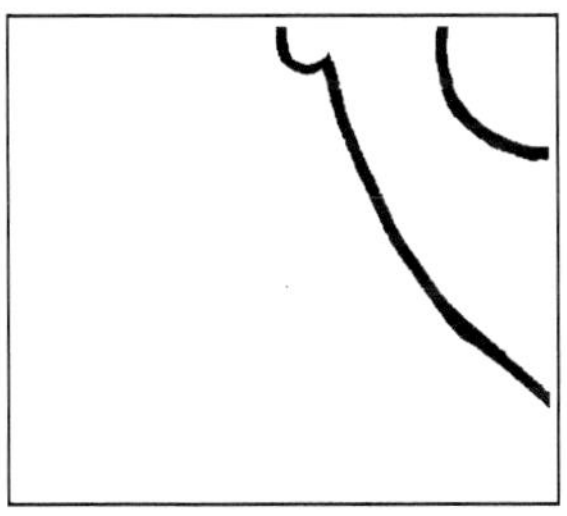

deux
neuf
trois
sept

neuf
sept
un
cinq

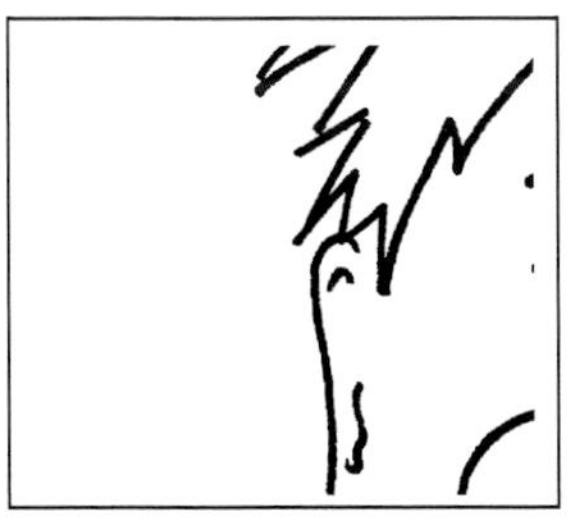

huit
sept
quatre
cinq

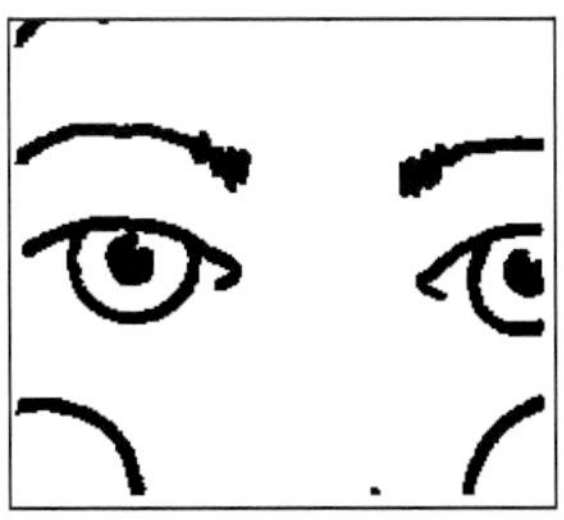

un
sept
quatre
cinq

Page 32 'le corps' – the body

Page 32 :1

Count & circle

Listen to the CD

Colorie et entoure la bonne image.

Colour and circle the correct picture.

This is a whole class activity and listening exercise.

Look at the picture and ask the children what action each member of the circus is doing.

The clown nodding his head is quite difficult to see.

Tapez du pied	Stamp your foot.
Frappez dans les mains.	Clap your hands.
Pliez les jambes.	Bend your knees. (la jambe – leg)
Levez le bras.	Put your hand up. (le bras – arm)
Bougez la tête.	Nod your head.

Page 32 :2

Observe and count in French

loto– bingo **NB When photocopying make sure the teacher has a copy so he/she can tick off the pictures as a reference.**

This is a revision exercise for parts of the body and numbers.
All the vocabulary is in picture form (no reading is required).
1st game: Ask the children to colour in 5 numbers.
Start reading out the numbers. 0 The children cross out the numbers they have coloured in.

The winner is the first child to cross out all 5 pictures.
This game can be played four times (2 x numbers 2 x vocab).

Page 32 :3

Observation in French

Drôle de corps! – Funny sort of body!

This is an activity for everyone.
Remind the children that **J'ai** – I have

1. Count the parts of the body and circle the correct number on the page.
2. When everyone has finished, you could ask them to read out a sentence at a time.

Game

Simon says

Jacques a dit Simon says

(This game is popular but it can get boring if played for too long.)

Jacques a dit **Tapez du pied**	Stamp your foot.
Jacques a dit **Frappez dans les mains.**	Clap your hands.
Jacques a dit **Pliez les jambes.**	Bend your knees. (la jambe – leg)
Jacques a dit **Levez le bras.**	Put your hand up. (le bras – arm)
Jacques a dit **Bougez la tête.**	Nod your head.

Why not try a variation?

Divide the class into five groups and give each group one action.
The teacher keeps a slow beat by tapping the table with his hand.
He calls out one of the actions and that group has to perform the action in time with the beat.
They keep going whilst another group is called and then another so at the end the whole class is performing their action in time to the beat!

Mon nom ....

le cirque

Circle the member of the circus as each instruction is read out.

Tapez du pied.	**Frappez dans les mains.**	**Pliez les jambes.**	**Levez le bras.**	**Bougez la tête.**
Stamp your foot	Clap your hands.	Bend your knees. (legs)	Put your hand (arm) up.	Nod your head.

Mon nom ....

loto

10	9	8	7	6	5	4	3	2	1
dix	neuf	huit	sept	six	cinq	quatre	trois	deux	un

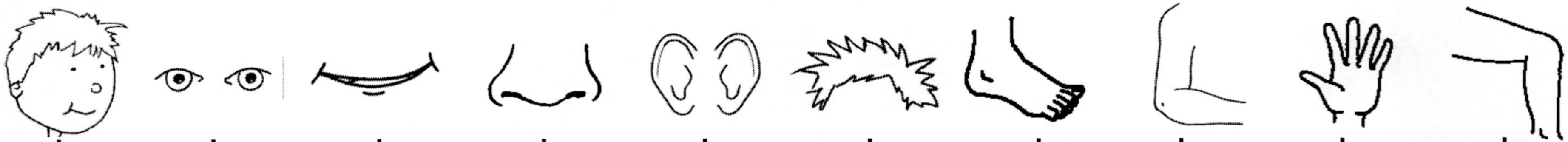

la tête	les yeux	la bouche	le nez	les oreilles	les cheveux	le pied	le bras	la main	la jambe

10	9	8	7	6	5	4	3	2	1
dix	neuf	huit	sept	six	cinq	quatre	trois	deux	un

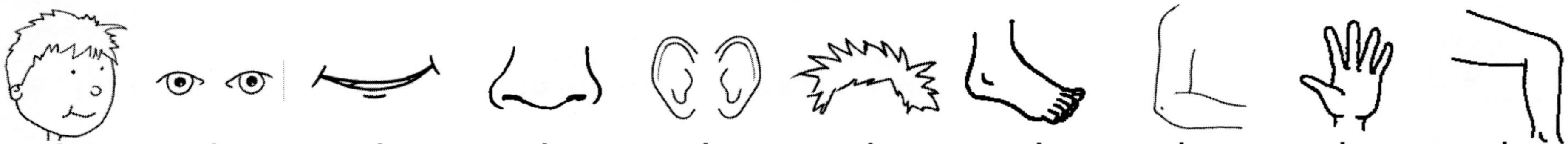

la tête	les yeux	la bouche	le nez	les oreilles	les cheveux	le pied	le bras	la main	la jambe

Mon nom ....

Drôle de corps!

Funny body!

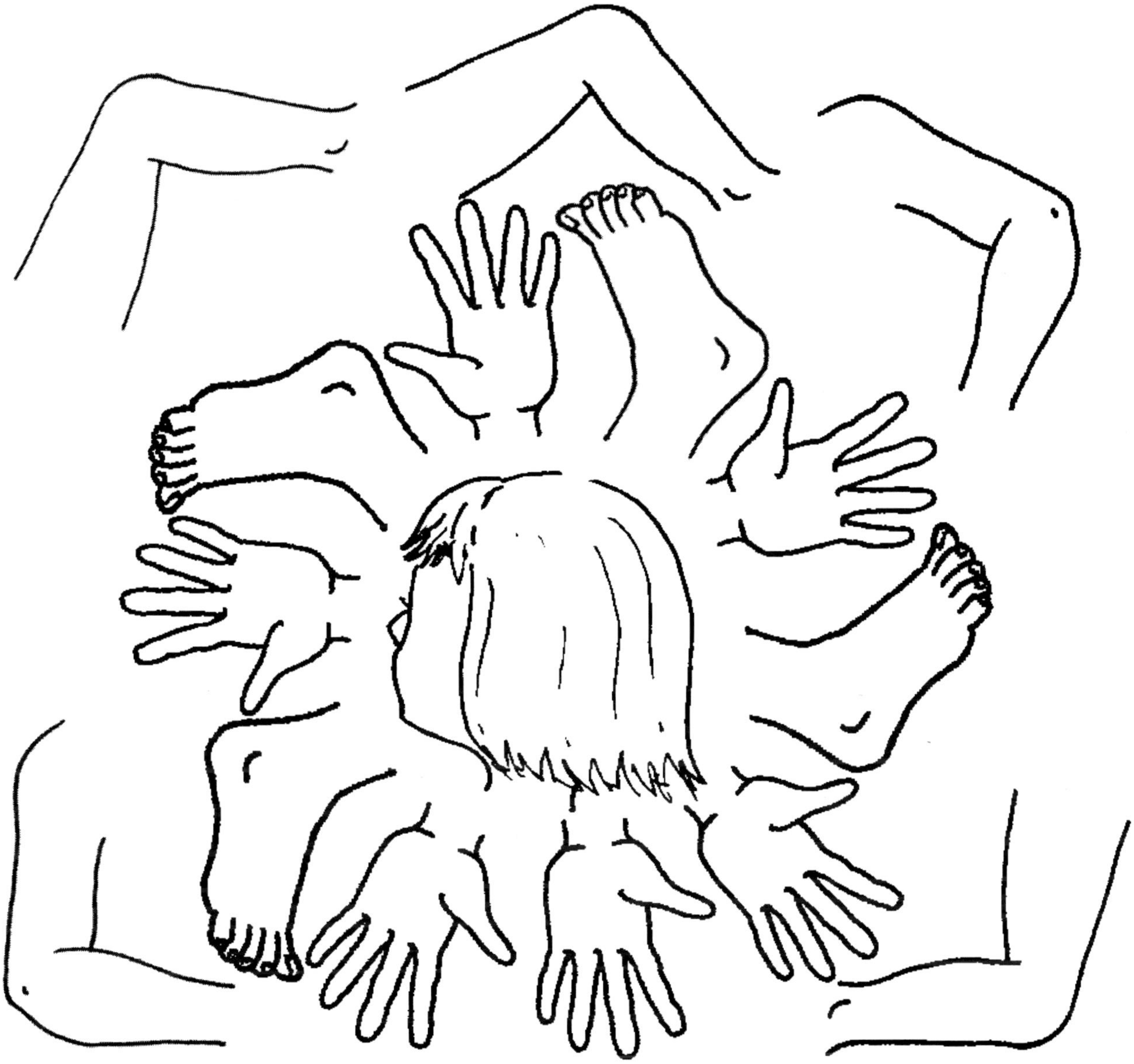

Entoure le bon chiffre.

Circle the correct number.

 **J'ai** une deux trois quatre cinq six **tête.**

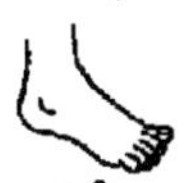 **J'ai** un deux trois quatre cinq six **pieds.**

 **J'ai** une deux trois quatre cinq six **mains.**

 **J'ai** un deux trois quatre cinq six **bras.**

 **J'ai** une deux trois quatre cinq six **jambes.**

Alouette

Alouette gentille Alouette Alouette je te plumerai

Je te plumerai la tête
Je te plumerai la tête
et la tête et la tête
Alouette Alouette
ahhhhh

Alouette gentille Alouette Alouette je te plumerai

Je te plumerai les ailes
Je te plumerai les ailes
et les ailes et les ailes
et la tête et la tête
Alouette Alouette
ahhhhh

Alouette gentille Alouette Alouette je te plumerai

Je te plumerai la queue
Je te plumerai la queue
et la queue et la queue
et les ailes et les ailes
et la tête et la tête
Alouette Alouette
ahhhhh

Alouette gentille Alouette Alouette je te plumerai

33:1 (Track 63 Karaoke version)

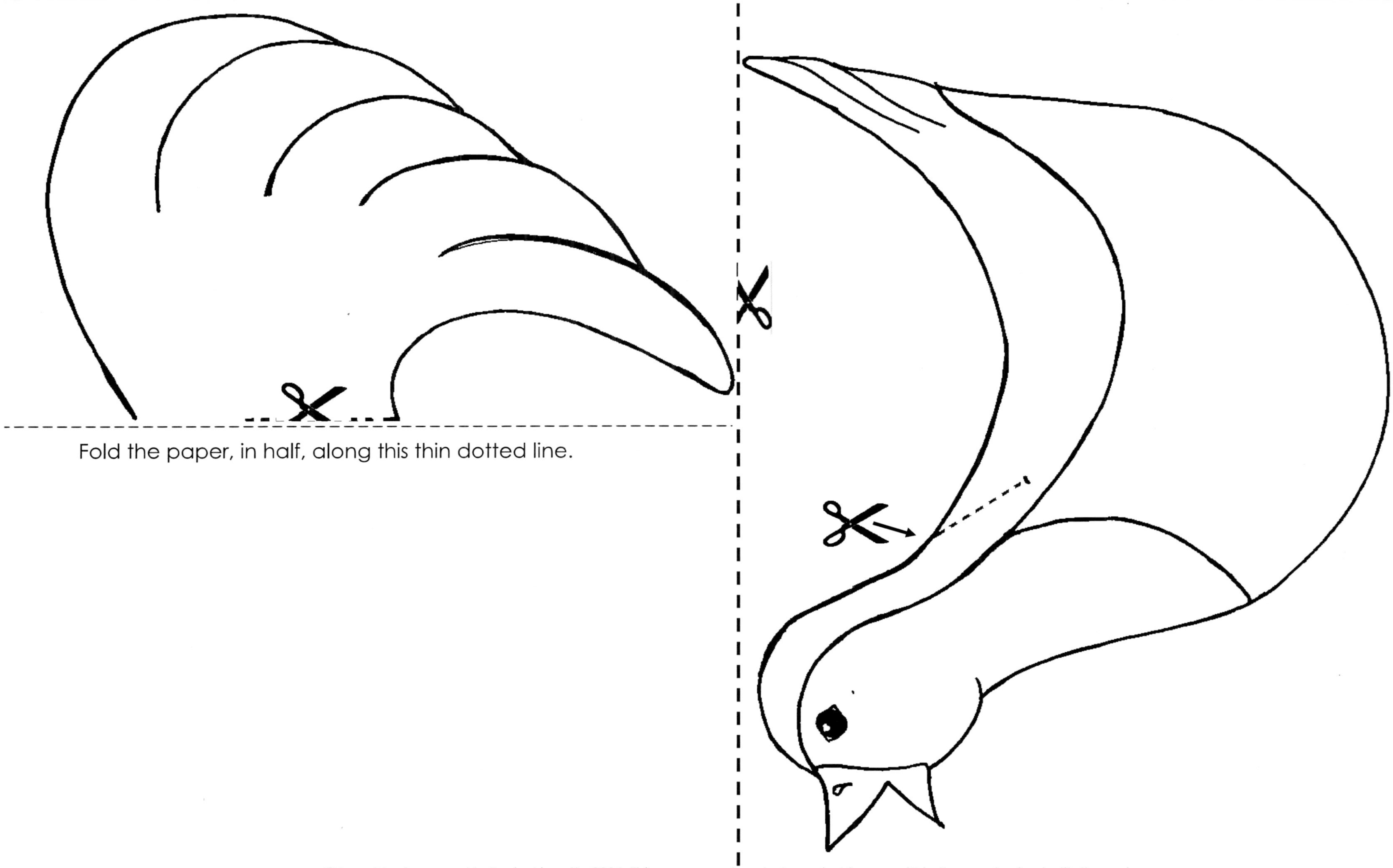
Fold the paper, in half, along this thin dotted line.

Page 34 'mes passe-temps' – my hobbies

Page 34 :1

My hobbies Listen to the CD

mes passe-temps – my hobbies

This is a listening game with a choice of hobbies.

Go over all the hobbies mentioned in this worksheet.

1. Listen to the CD and colour in the hobby each child likes.

CD Script

Lucas aime la natation.
Jade aime la télévision.
Emma aime la cuisine.
Clément aime le football.
Camille aime la lecture.

Ask questions: ie **"Qui aime la cuisine?"** Who likes cooking?
Answer **"Emma aime la cuisine."** Emma likes cooking.

Page 34 :2

Picture association

Forme des paires – Make pairs

This exercise is for the children who find writing easy.

All they have to do is write the correct number associated with the hobby and write the name of the hobby in French.
eg The boy swimming is **1** – associated with water **1**

All worksheets marked **:2** should be completed neatly and accurately.

Page 34 :3

Craft

Making a booklet

Making a booklet

1. Cut along the dotted line so the paper is in two halves.
2. Stick the edge of page deux (2) with the edge of page trois (3).

   You can keep the 6 pictures as a freize or fold them (fan like) into a booklet.

   Make sure the page numbers run consecutively.

   See if the children can read the pages of their little booklets (including the page numbers)

Choosing time

Choosing time

Traditional French Songs	**3, 17, 33, 42**
Skoldo French Songs	**7, 10, 13, 20, 23, 27, 30, 37, 46, 51, 54**
Miming	**21, 22, 29,**
Simon says	**31, 32**
Felt games	**4, 11, 14, 19, 28**
Vegetable chant + actions	**25**
"The fox in the house" chant	**18**

Mon nom ....

mes passe-temps

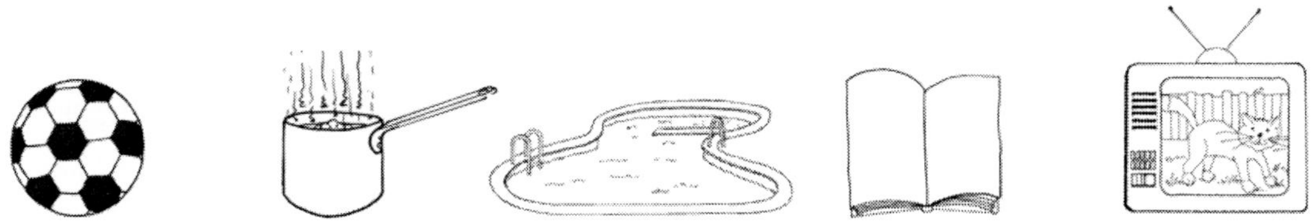

le **football** la **cuisine** la **natation** la **lecture** la **télévision**

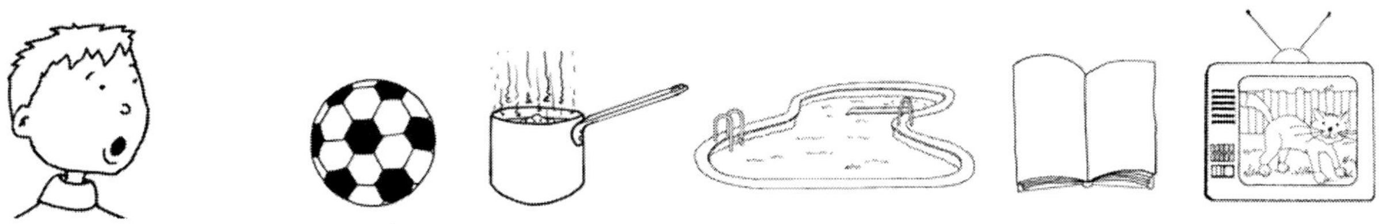

Lucas

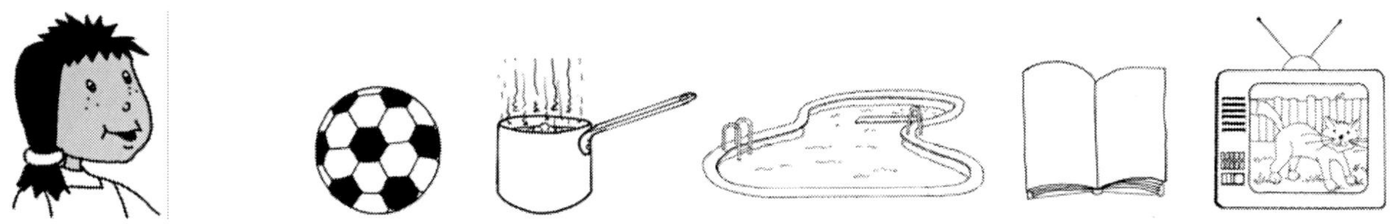

Jade

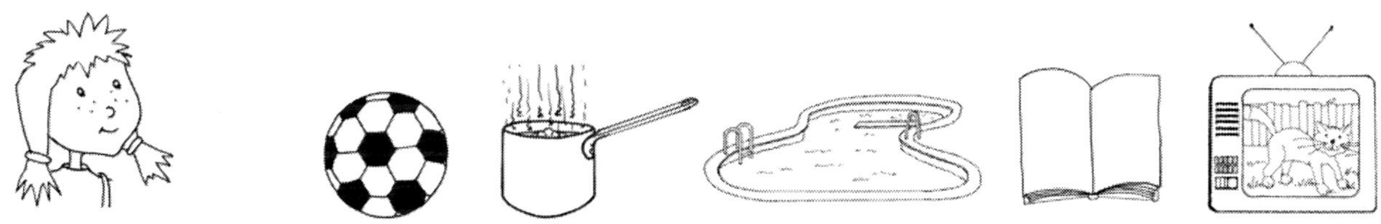

Emma

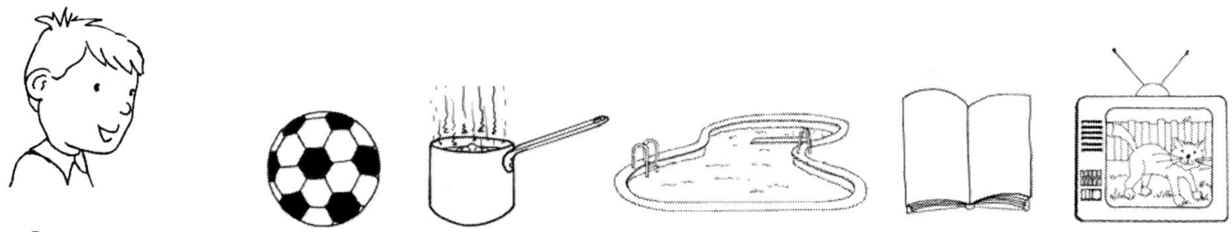

Clément

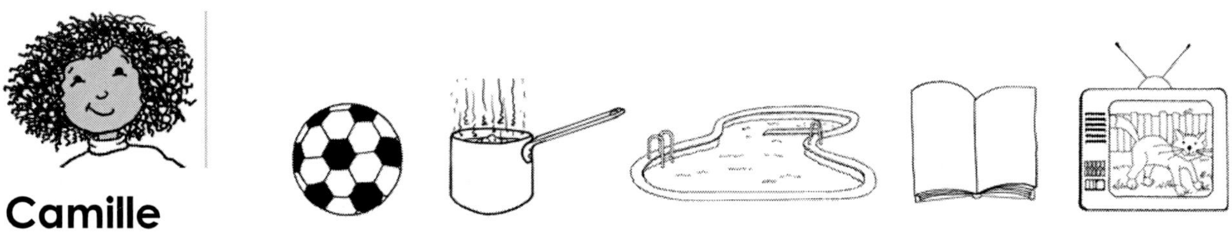

Camille

Mon nom ....

Forme des paires

le **football**

la **cuisine**

la **natation**

la **lecture**

la **télévision**

1

la ....

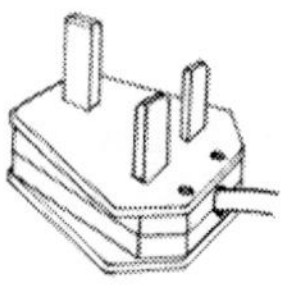
2

le ....

3

la ....

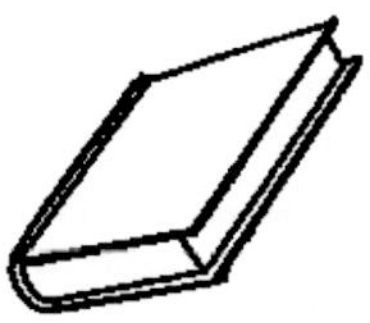
4

la ....

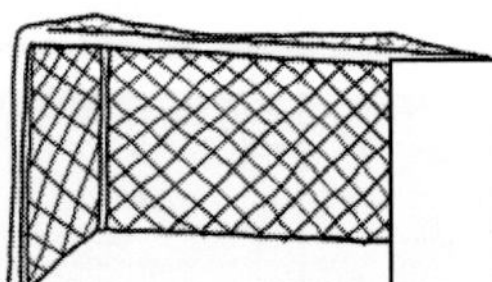
5

la ....

mes passe-temps

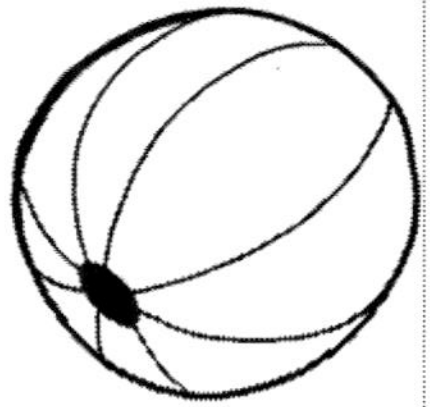

Mon nom ....

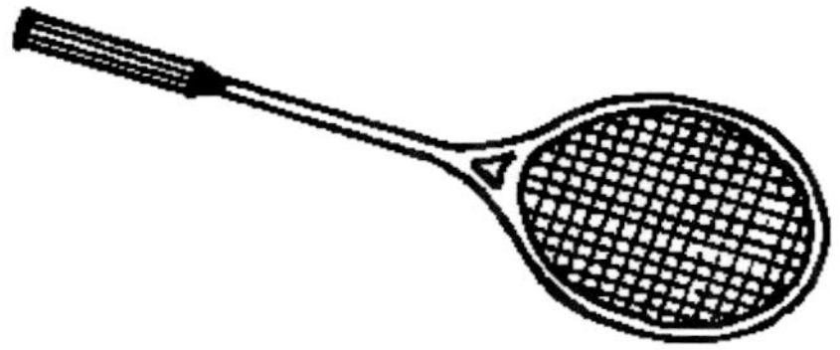

J'aime la télévision

un

J'aime la lecture

deux

J'aime la natation

trois

J'aime le football

quatre

J'aime la cuisine

cinq

Page 35 'les jouets' – toys

Page 35 :1

My hobbies Listen to the CD

les jouets – toys

This is a listening activity learning about vowels.

Go over all the words and pick out the vowels.
Don't forget that **y** is a vowel in French.
There are six vowels in French: **a e (é) i o u y**
Vowels with accents have their own pronunciation.

CD Script

le livre	**e i e**
le nounours	**e o u o u**
la poupée	**a o u é e**
le ballon	**e a o**
le jeu vidéo	**e e u i é o**

Page 35 :2

Word search in French

les jouets – toys

This wordsearch can be used for able writers and early learners.

1. The able writers need to copy the words on the dotted lines.
2. The less fluent writers need only find the words in the wordsearch.

For those who like colouring, each letter used in the wordsearch can be coloured in.
For those who don't like colouring, they can design patterns in the boxes where the letters are found.

Page 35 :3

Beware of the cauliflowers

Attention aux choux-fleurs! – Beware of the cauliflowers!

This is a dice game.
Fold the paper along the dotted line. One side for each game.

The teacher throws a dice and reads out the number followed by the French for the picture in the box.

The aim of the game is to colour in (very quickly) all the pictures before three 6s (the cauliflowers) have been thrown.

If you can get each child to throw the dice and play the game this way, it is more exciting but less controllable!

Game

Simon says

Jacques a dit Simon says

Jacques a dit touche la tête	(touch your head)
Jacques a dit touche les yeux	(touch your eyes)
Jacques a dit touche les oreilles	(touch your ears)
Jacques a dit touche la bouche	(touch your mouth)
Jacques a dit touche le nez	(touch your nose)
Jacques a dit touche les cheveux	(touch your hair)

When **you say Jacques a dit** ✓you must obey the command
When **you don't say Jacques a dit** × you don't obey the command

Mon nom ……………………………………

Colorie les voyelles

les voyelles a e é i o u y

le livre

le nounours

la poupée

le ballon

le jeu vidéo

Mon nom ....

les jouets

b	z	p	l	e	j	n
a	d	o	a	t	e	o
l	g	u	s	y	u	u
l	k	p	m	u	v	n
o	j	é	d	j	i	o
n	m	e	x	e	d	u
r	k	r	a	n	é	r
l	i	v	r	e	o	s

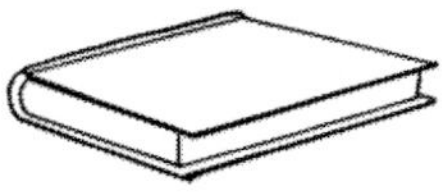

le **livre**

le ....

le **nounours**

le ....

la **poupée**

la ....

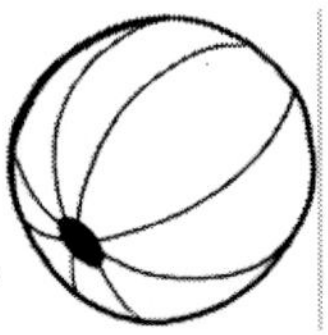

le **ballon**

le ....

le **jeu vidéo**

le ....

....

Mon nom ....

Attention aux choux-fleurs!

Page 36 'Où habites-tu?' – Where do you live?

Page 36 :1

Où habites-tu?

Listen to the CD

Où habites-tu? – Where do you live?

Introduce the question " Où habites-tu ?"

Ask a few children where they live and get them to reply "J'habite à ... ."

Listen to the CD and look at the picture.

CD Script

Où habites-tu, Patrice? J'habite à Banville.
Où habites-tu, Gilbert? J'habite à Courset.
Où habites-tu, Emilie? J'habite à Chassant.
Où habites-tu, Hubert? J'habite à St Michel.
Où habites-tu, Sophie? J'habite à Vernon.

The children can colour in the picture listening to track 37 of the **CD**.
This will introduce them to the next Skoldo song "C'est mon anniversaire."

Page 36 :2

Where do you live?

Où habites-tu?

Look at the six different children, their names and the symbols.

Ask the question " Où habites-tu?"

Write the correct place on the dotted line next to each child's picture. The symbols and places are found at the top of the page.

Revise al the questions and answers covered so far in the book.
Comment tu t'appelles? Page 16
Quel âge as-tu? Page 26
Où habites-tu?

Page 36 :3

Spot the difference

Trouve les 10 différences – Spot the difference

1. The missing giraffe picture
2. The octopus' shoe
3. The octopus' eye
4. The card held by the octopus
5. The suckers on the octopus' tentacle
6. The pleats on the elephant's skirt
7. The teacher's arm
8. The belt on the teacher's dress
9. The tip of the hedgehog's nose
10. The ears on the mouse's picture

"How are you?"

song + actions

Ça va?

This song and its actions are fully explained on page 45

It is worth learning this little activity song at this stage and revise it often as the spoken French is useful.

The children might start getting confused with the different questions and answers but lots of practice will soon sort them out!

Mon nom ....

Où habites-tu?

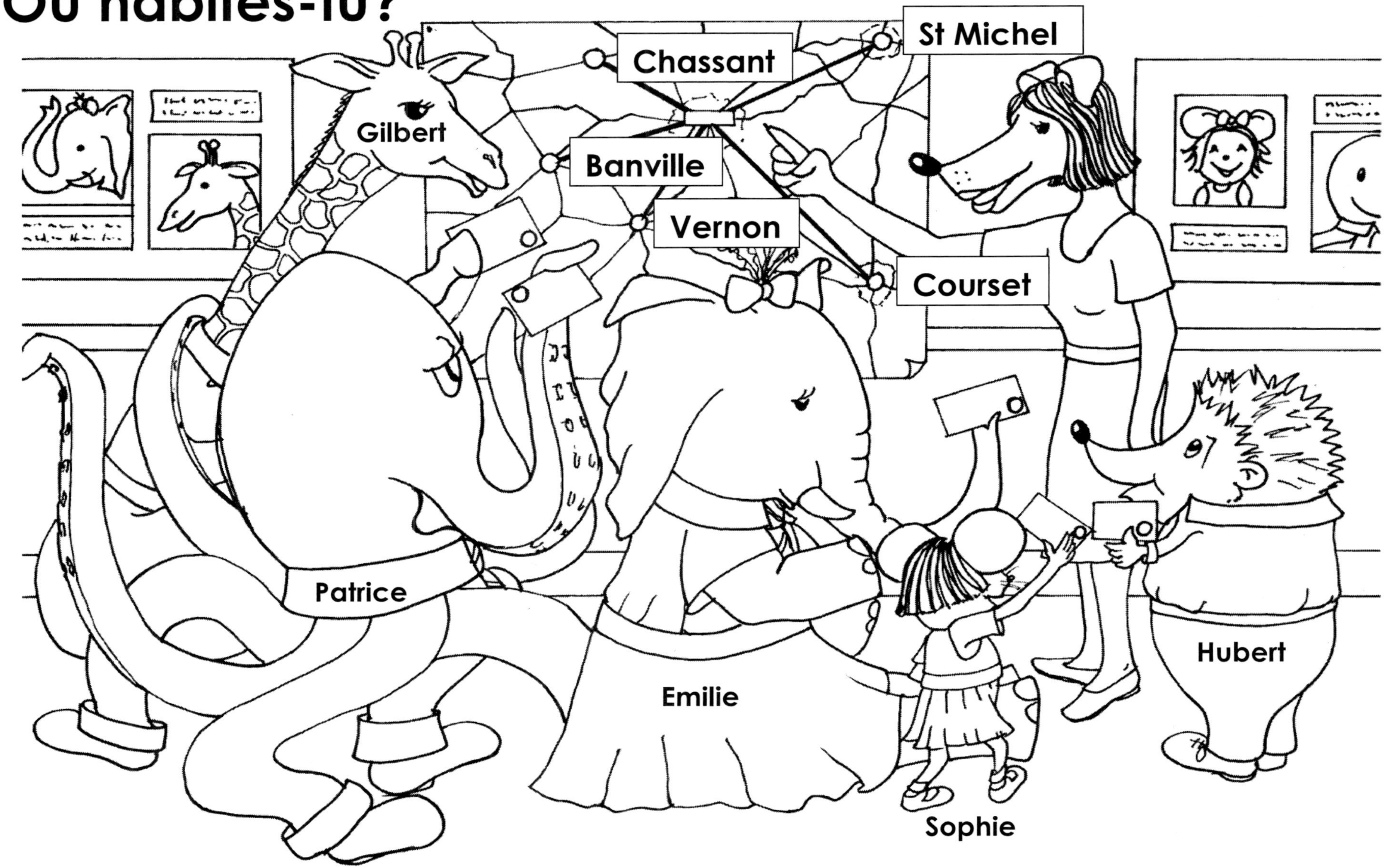

Mon nom ……………………………………

Où habites-tu?

Write the name of the village where each child lives on the dotted line.

St Michel **Courset** **Banville** **Chassant** **Vernon**

J'habite à …………………………………… .

J'habite à …………………………………… .

J'habite à …………………………………… .

J'habite à …………………………………… .

J'habite à …………………………………… .

J'habite à …………………………………… .

Mon nom ....

Trouve les 10 différences

C'est mon anniversaire

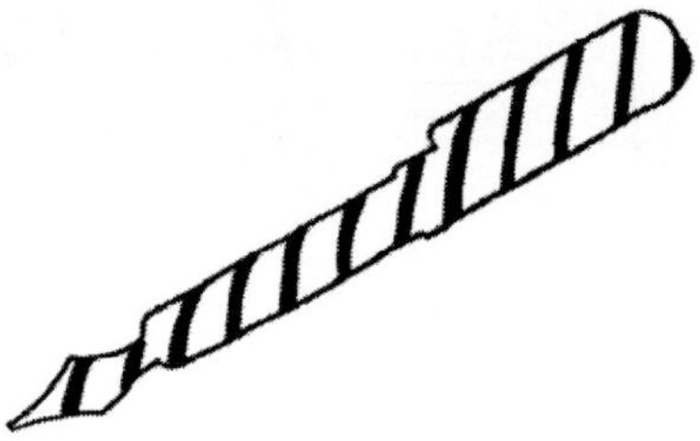

Aujourd'hui, j'ai trois cadeaux
Aujourd'hui, j'ai trois cadeaux
Aujourd'hui, j'ai trois cadeaux
C'est mon anniversaire

Aujourd'hui, j'ai un lapin
Aujourd'hui, j'ai un lapin
Aujourd'hui, j'ai un lapin
C'est mon anniversaire

Aujourd'hui, j'ai un nounours
Aujourd'hui, j'ai un nounours
Aujourd'hui, j'ai un nounours
C'est mon anniversaire

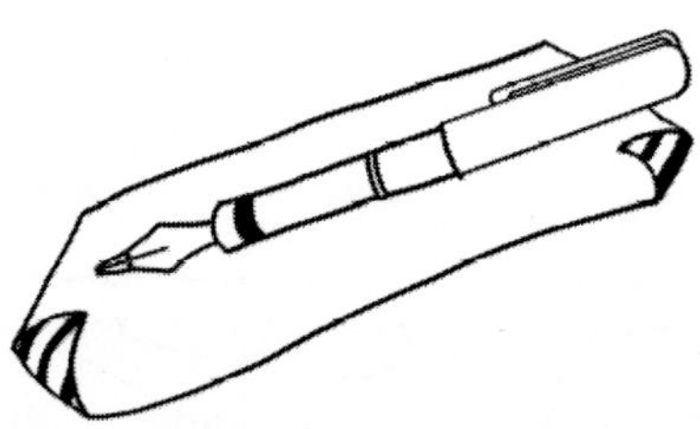

Aujourd'hui, j'ai un stylo
Aujourd'hui, j'ai un stylo
Aujourd'hui, j'ai un stylo
C'est mon anniversaire

37:1 (Track 64 Karaoke version)

joyeux anniversaire

Page 38 'le magasin de jouets' – toy shop

Page 38 :1

toy shop

Listen to the CD

le magasin de jouets – toy shop

This is a relaxing lesson based on colouring and observation.

TIP: It is a good idea just to add a small dot of colour in the correct place when following the CD instructions.
(This keeps everyone at the same pace.)

CD Script

Colorie le nounours en marron.
Colour the teddy brown.

Colorie les poupées en bleu, rose et jaune.
Colour the dolls blue, pink and yellow.

Colorie les livres en violet, jaune, rouge et vert.
Colour the books purple, yellow, red and green.

Colorie le gros ballon en vert et rose.
Colour the large ball green and pink.

Colorie le petit ballon en orange et bleu.
Colour the small ball orange and blue.

Colorie les boîtes en violet et en rouge.
Colour the boxes purple and red.

Page 38 :2

Do you have a ...?

Tu as un/une ...? Do you have a ...?

Look at the six children, their names and their possessions.

Ask the question " Tu as un/une ....?"

Write the correct word on the line next to each child's picture.

Revise all the questions and answers covered so far in the book.

Comment tu t'appelles?	Page 16	Quel âge as-tu?	Page 26
Où habites-tu?	Page 36		

Page 38 :3

Spot the difference

Trouve les 10 différences – Spot the difference

1. The teddy's nose
2. The teddy's arm
3. The stripes on the ball
4. The middle doll's collar
5. The top circle on the large ball
6. The star on the little ball
7. The top book on the pile
8. The oval shape on the book
9. The picture of saturn on the toy box
10. The word 'Monopoly'

The felt game

As-tu le bleu? Have you got the blue? Children sit in a circle

Take ten coloured felt squares and whilst singing '**Frère Jacques**' get the children to pass the felts round in a circle.

On the last word of the song (dong) the children with the felt squares sit on them (the others pretend to do the same).

Children take it in turns to ask each other "As-tu le (whatever colour)?" until the correct child has been asked.

Keep going until all the colours have been discovered.

Mon nom ....

le magasin de jouets

Mon nom ....

Tu as......?

Write the French for the toy/book each child has in his/her bedroom.

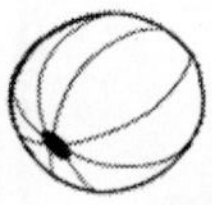

une **poupée** un **ballon** un **livre** un **jeu vidéo** un **nounours**

 **Oui, j'ai quatre (4)** ....s.

 **Oui, j'ai deux (2)** ....s.

 **Oui, j'ai un (1)** ....

 **Oui, j'ai trois (3)** ....s.

 **Oui, j'ai un (1)** ....

 **Oui, j'ai cinq (5)** ....s.

Mon nom ....

Trouve les 10 différences

Page 39 'les révisions' – revision

Page 39 :1

Listen and colour

Listen to the CD

Écoute et colorie – Listen and colour

This is a whole class activity and listening exercise.

Go over all the vocabulary before listening to the CD.

Write the correct number in the correct box.

1. La natation est numéro quatre.
2. Le nounours est numéro neuf.
3. La cuisine est numéro six.
4. Le football est numéro dix.
5. La poupée est numéro trois.
6. La lecture est numéro sept.
7. Le jeu vidéo est numéro deux.
8. La télévision est numéro huit.
9. Le livre est numéro un.
10. Le ballon est numéro cinq.

Page 39 :2

Observe in French

loto– bingo **NB When photocopying make sure the teacher has a copy so he/she can tick off the pictures as a reference.**

This is a revision exercise for hobbies, toys and colours.
All the vocabulary is in picture form (no reading is required).
1st game: Ask the children to colour in 5 colours codes.
Start reading out the colours slowly one by one.
The children cross out the colour codes they have coloured in when the teacher reads it out.

The winner is the first child to cross out all 5 pictures.

This game can be played four times (2 x numbers 2 x vocab).

Page 39 :3

Observation in French

Colorie les paires – Colour the pairs

This is an activity for everyone.

1. Look at the shapes.
2. Find the small sample of each shape and colour that shape in its correct colour.

Miming

Hobby and activities

Miming

Divide the class into 10 groups.

Take 10 pieces of paper and draw one of the hobbies or activities shown on the loto sheet, on each piece.
You could cut out the pictures from the loto sheet if you prefer.

Hand out one piece of paper to each group.

Each group discusses how it is going to act out the hobby/activity in front of the others.

One by one, a group stands in front of the class and acts out their word.

The rest of the class has to guess, in French, what is drawn on the piece of paper.

Mon nom ....

Écoute et colorie

1	2	3	4	5
le livre	le jeu vidéo	la poupée	la natation	le ballon
6	7	8	9	10
la cuisine	la lecture	la télévision	le nounours	le football

✍ Mon nom ....

loto

jaune	bleu	vert	marron	blanc	rouge	orange	violet	noir	rose

la natation	la lecture	le ballon	la télévision	le nounours	le livre	le jeu vidéo	la cuisine	la poupée	le football

jaune	bleu	vert	marron	blanc	rouge	orange	violet	noir	rose

la natation	la lecture	le ballon	la télévision	le nounours	le livre	le jeu vidéo	la cuisine	la poupée	le football

Mon nom ....

Trouve et colorie les paires

Find and colour the identical shapes looking at the clues at the bottom of the page.

 **rouge**

 **marron**

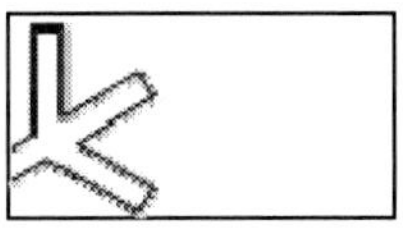 **bleu**

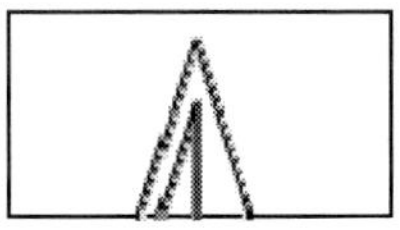 **rose**

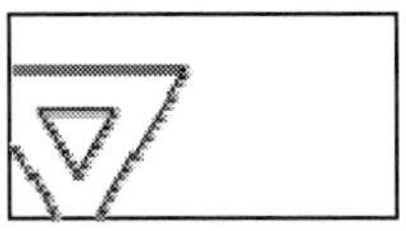 **jaune**

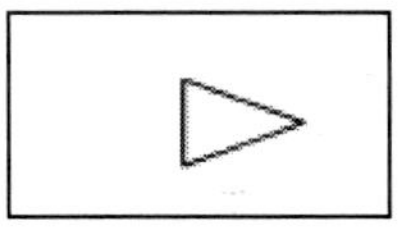 **gris**

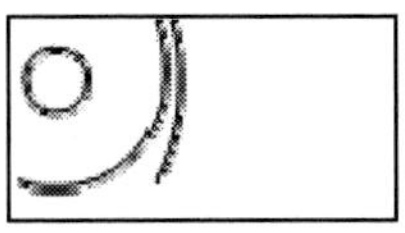 **violet**

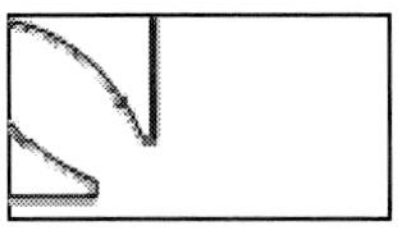 **vert**

Page 40 'la campagne (i)' – the countryside

Page 40 :1

Colour the consonants

Listen to the CD

Colorie les consonnes – Colour the consonants

This is a listening activity learning about consonants.

Go over all the words and pick out the consonants.
Don't forget that **y** isn't a consonant in French.
There are 20 consonants in French:

b c d f g h j k l m n p q r s t v w x z

1. Listen to the CD and colour the consonants as they are read out.

CD Script

la fleur	**l f l r**
la rivière	**l r v r**
le papillon	**l p p l l n**
le pont	**l p n t**
l'arbre	**l r b r**

Page 40 :2

Maths in French

Compte, calcule et écris – Count, add and write.

This exercise is ideal for children who find writing and maths easy.

They need to look up the number which goes with each picture, add or subtract the numbers and write the new number in the answer section, drawing its picture in the box.

Worksheets marked **:2** should be completed neatly & accurately.

six (ladybird) **neuf** (flower) **huit** (hare) **dix** (tree) **sept** (cobweb)

Page 40 :3

Craft

Making a Caterpillar

Craft! – Making a caterpillar

This is a chance to do some craft although it does need preparation.

1. Cut out 13 strips of green paper/card as if making paper chains.
2. Cut out one oval shape.
3. Make each strip of paper into a circular shape and link them all together in a chain.

When the chain is complete, stick the head on the last link.
Tying green wool to the head enables the caterpillar to dance.

Game

Simon says

Jacques a dit touche… Simon says touch …

Jacques a dit touche la tête	(touch your head)
Jacques a dit touche les yeux	(touch your eyes)
Jacques a dit touche les oreilles	(touch your ears)
Jacques a dit touche la bouche	(touch your mouth)
Jacques a dit touche le nez	(touch your nose)
Jacques a dit touche les cheveux	(touch your hair)

When you start with **Jacques a dit** ✓you obey the command
When you **don't** start with **Jacques a dit** × you don't obey the command

Mon nom ....

Colorie les consonnes

les **consonnes** **b c d f g h j k l m n p q r s t v w x z**

 la fleur

 la rivière

 le papillon

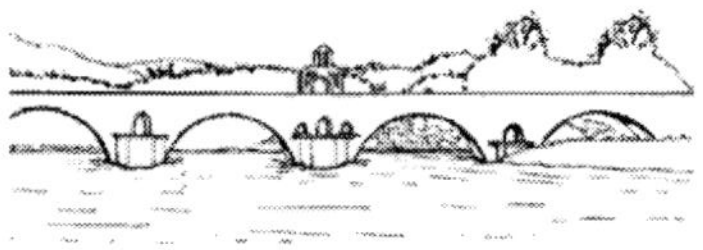 le pont

 l'arbre

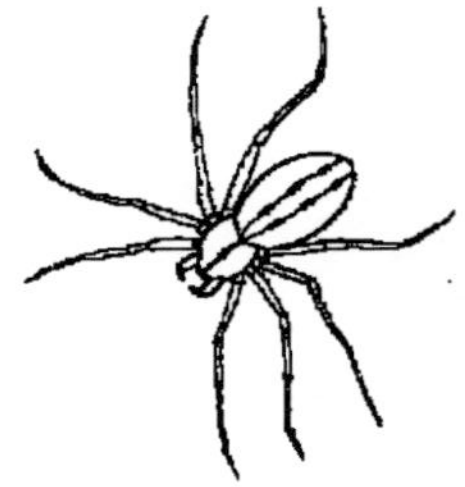

Mon nom ....

Compte, calcule et écris

un	deux	trois	quatre	cinq	six	sept	huit	neuf	dix

_ _ _ _ – _ _ _ _ _ = _ _ _

_ _ _ _ + _ _ _ _ = _ _ _ _

_ _ _ _ + _ _ _ _ _ = _ _ _ _

_ _ _ + _ _ _ _ _ _ = _ _ _

_ _ _ _ – _ _ = _ _ _ _

fabrique une chenille

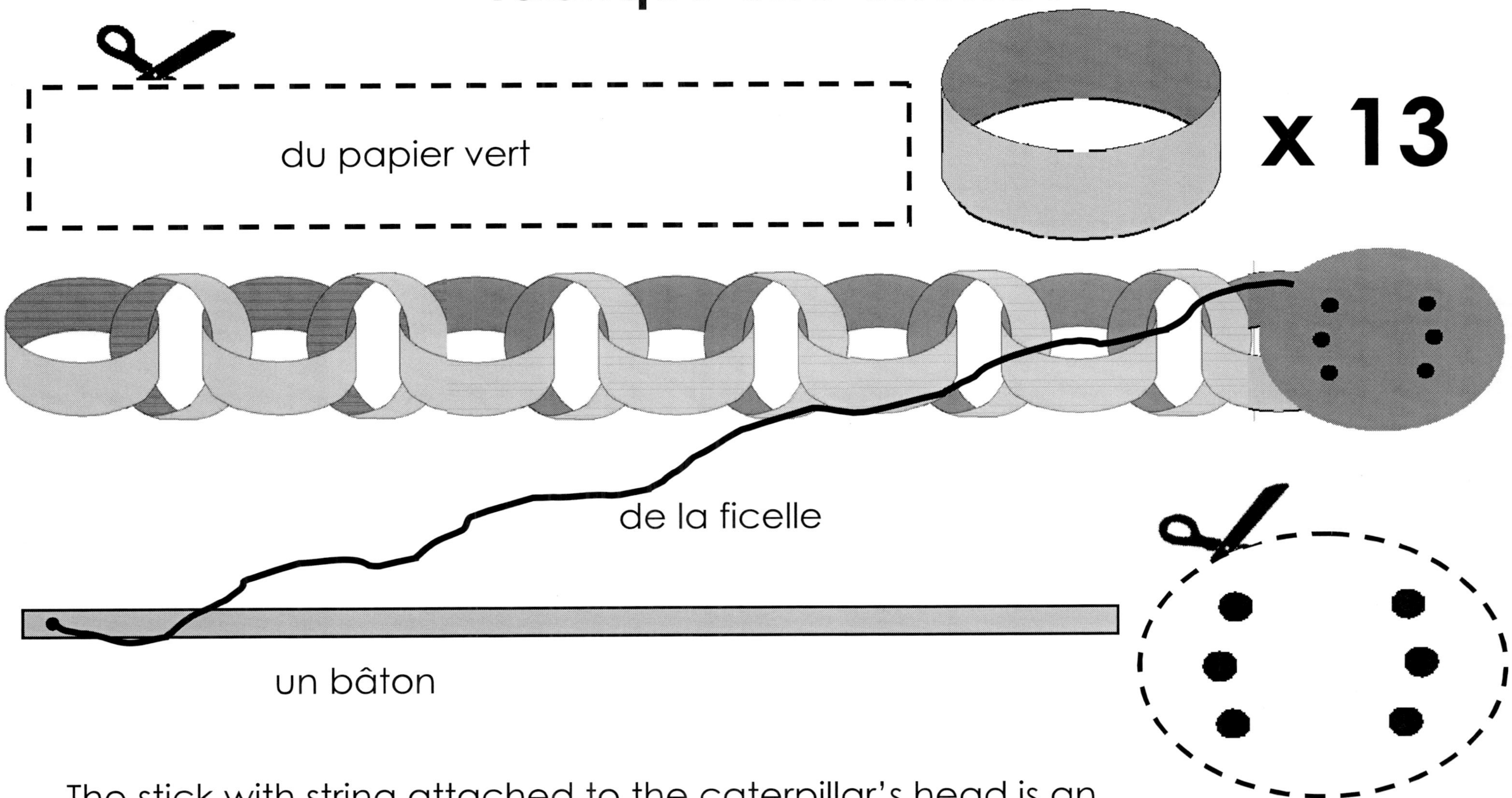

The stick with string attached to the caterpillar's head is an optional extra enabling the caterpillar's head and body to move. Using green paper gives the caterpillar a more realistic look.

Page 41 'la campagne (ii)' – the countryside

Page 41 :1

Where are the animals?

Listen to the CD

Où sont les animaux? – Where are the animals?

This is a listening activity learning about the preposition **dans** (in).

Go over the vocabulary at the top of the page as well as the animals and colours.

le renard	the fox	le hérisson	the hedgehog		
le lièvre	the hare	la souris	the mouse	la taupe	the mole

1. Colour the animals in their correct colour.
   Blanche is the feminine of blanc (mouse is feminine in French)
   Noire is the feminine of noir (mole is feminine in French)
2. Listen to the CD and circle the place where each animal is hiding.

CD Script

Le renard rouge est dans la valise.
Le hérrison marron est dans la boîte.
Le lièvre gris est dans le garage.
La souris blanche est dans le placard.
La taupe noire est dans le tiroir.

Page 41 :2

Recognize of wild animals in French

Cherche les animaux – Look for the animals.

This exercise helps children recognize our countryside animals.

Ask the children to describe each of the five animals.
Point out the distinctive marks of each animal.

1. prickles	hedgehog
2. bushy tail with white tip	fox
3. large floppy ears/hind legs	hare
4. large digging paws/blind	mole
5. long thin tail	mouse

Page 41 :3

Craft

Making a Caterpillar

Craft! – Making a caterpillar

1. Revise the vowels and the consonants with the children and colour the alphabet letters correctly.
2. Revise 'Comment tu t'appelles?' 'Je m'appelle...'
3. Colour the snake and then cut him out.

Game

Animal Drawing

Animal drawing game

1. Hand out a piece of paper to each child.
2. Draw VERY simply on the board, the distinctive markings of each of the five wild animals.
3. Ask the children to choose one of the animals and copy its distinctive marking.
4. Call out one of the animals, in French, and the children who have drawn that animal hold up their pieces of paper and win a point.

Mon nom ....

Où sont les animaux?

la boîte le placard la valise le tiroir le garage

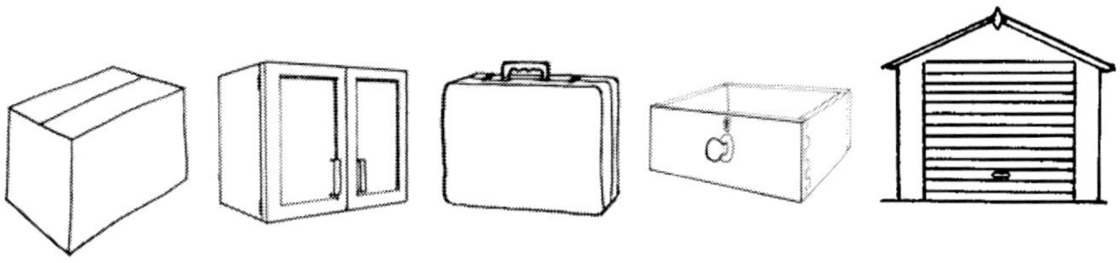

rouge

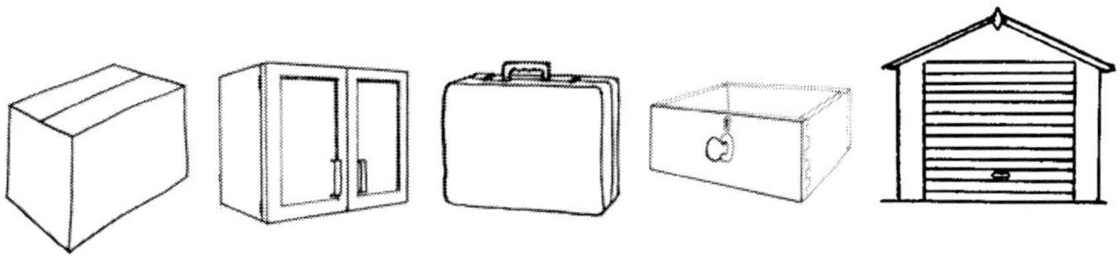

marron

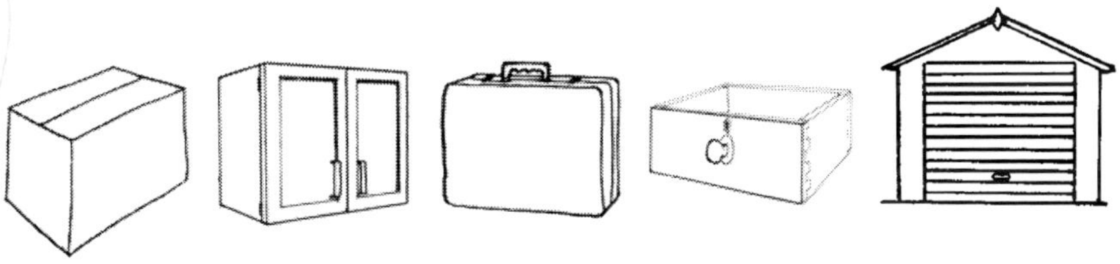

gris

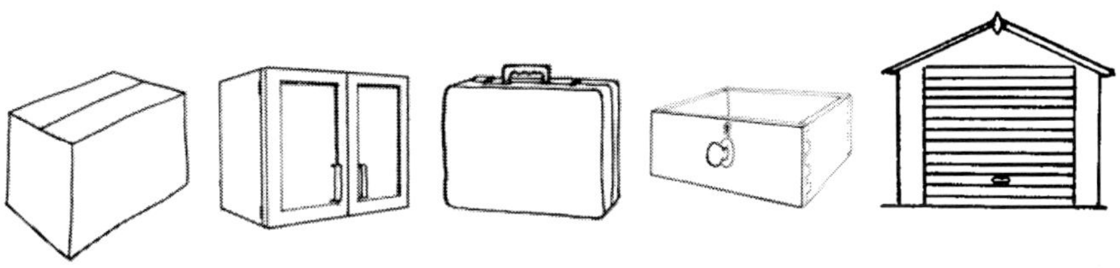

blanche

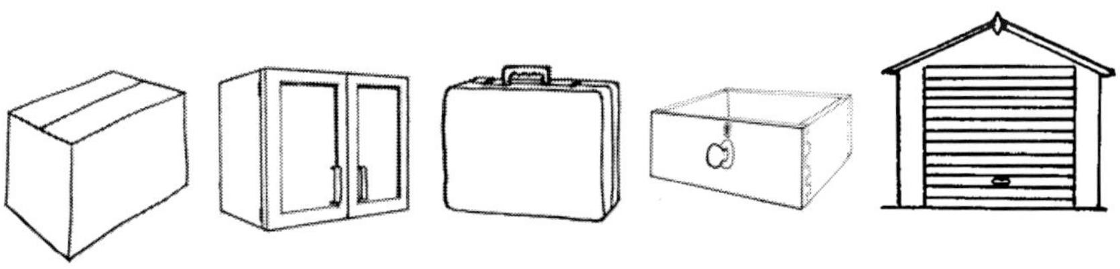

noire

Mon nom ....

Cherche les animaux

le **renard**

le **hérisson**

le **lièvre**

la **souris**

la **taupe**

le ....

le ....

le ....

la ....

la ....

Find the five animals in the following lines of letters . (One animal in each row)

pvhérissonputjkwqs

gpbhgcxzjwrenardv

wxslièvrekjhgfdsnbp

csbpouytaupekvwq

xkpdfxbmnjhsourisn

Fabrique un serpent

Colorie les **voyelles** en bleu

a e i o u y

Colorie les **consonnes** en rouge

b c d f g h j k l m

n p q r s t v w x z

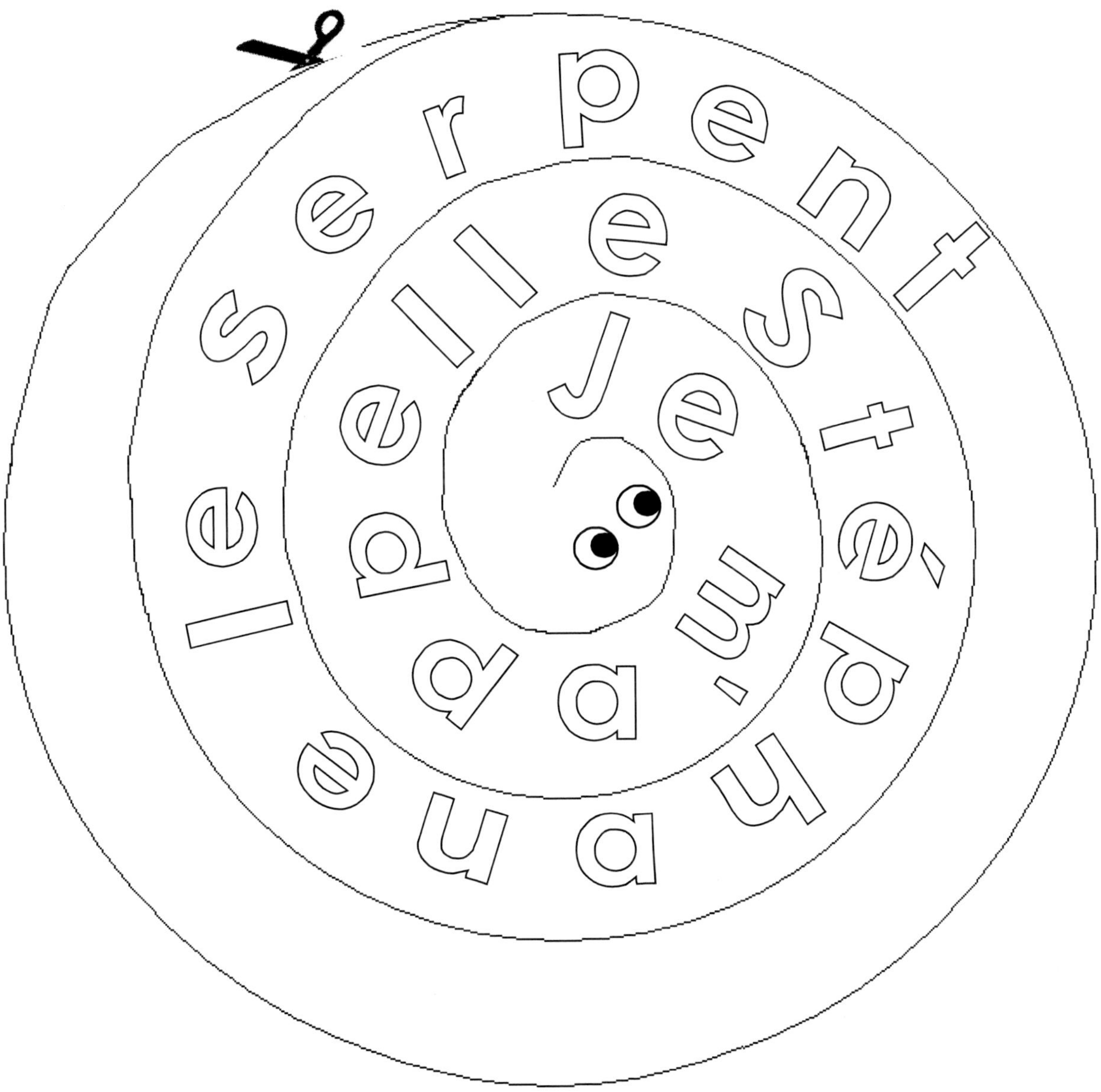

Sur le pont d'Avignon

Refrain: Sur le pont d'Avignon On y danse, on y danse
Sur le pont d'Avignon On y danse tout en rond

les beaux messieurs
font comme ça
et puis encore
comme ça (Refrain)

les belles dames
font comme ça
et puis encore
comme ça (Refrain)

TO MAKE A BOAT

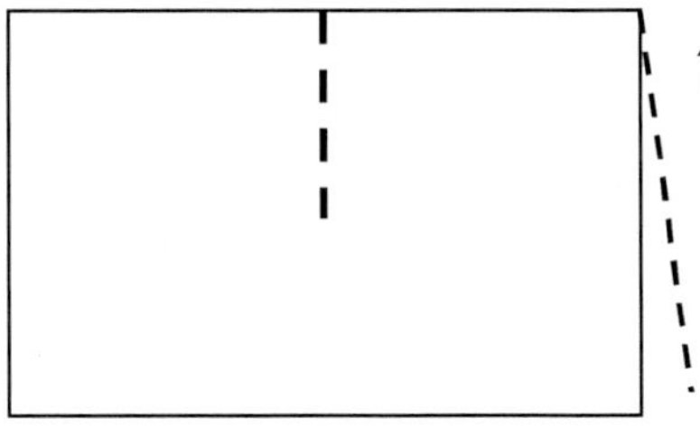

1. Fold A4 paper in half from portrait to landscape.

Find the centre line by folding the left side onto the right side.

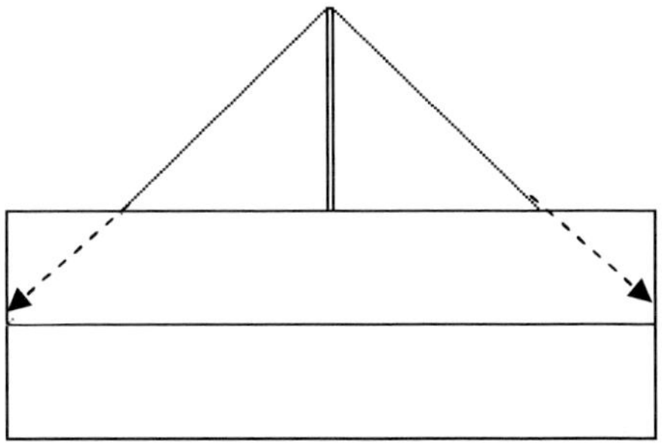

2. Find the centre line and fold the two corners into the centre.

Then fold the top of the two strips of paper upwards.

Don't forget **3.**

3. Fold the two small triangles backwards so they disappear.

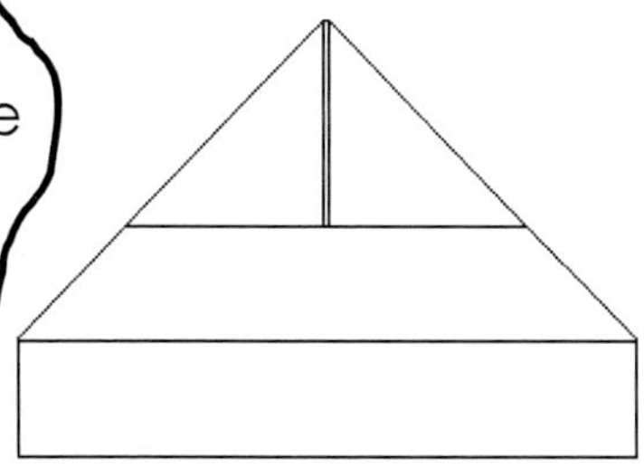

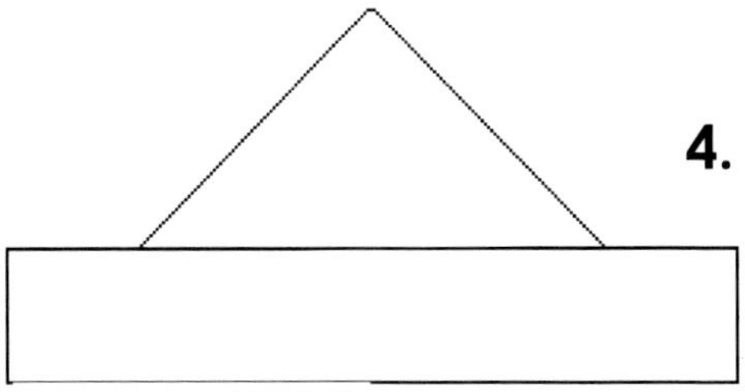

4. Turn the paper over and fold the other lower strip upwards.
You have made a hat shape.

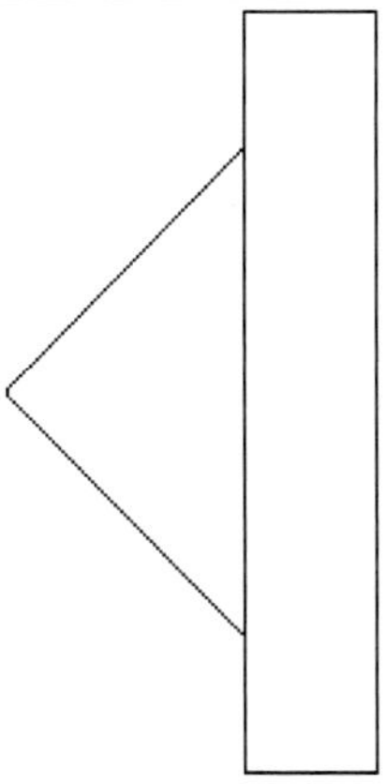

5. Turn 90° and open it.

With the thumbs inside, lay the upper and lower parts of the hat onto each other.

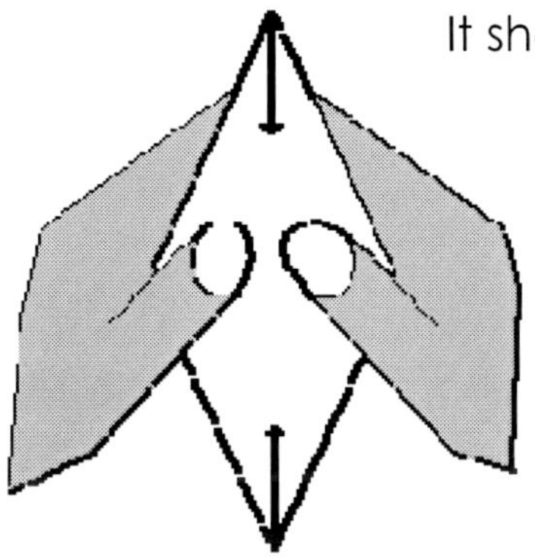

It should look like this.

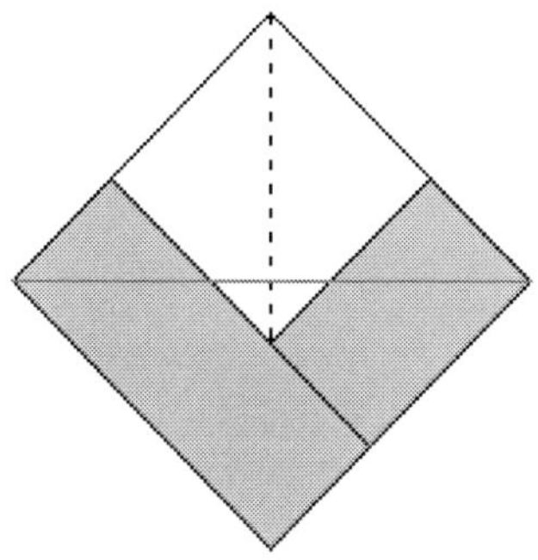

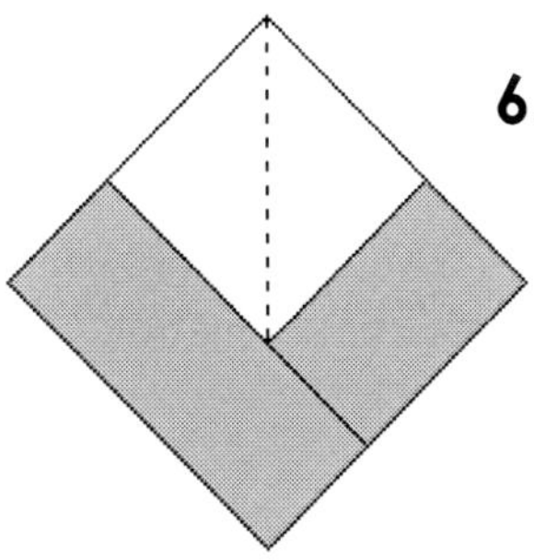

6. Fold the lower front triangle upwards. It should look like **B**.

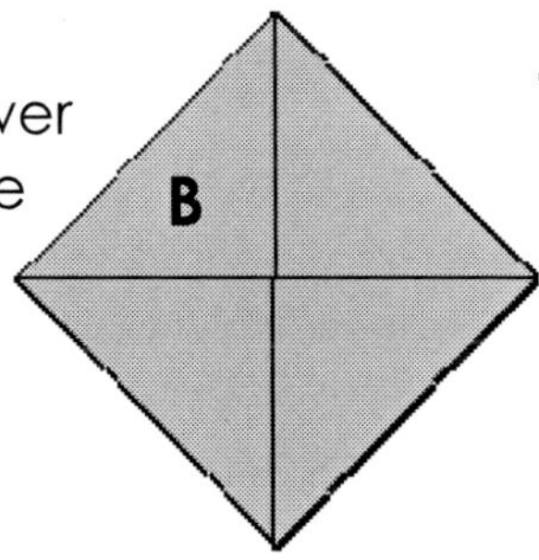

7. Turn the paper over and fold up the other lower triangle.

You have a hat without a rim.

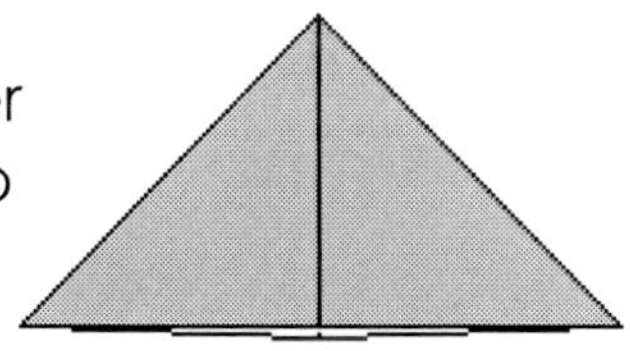

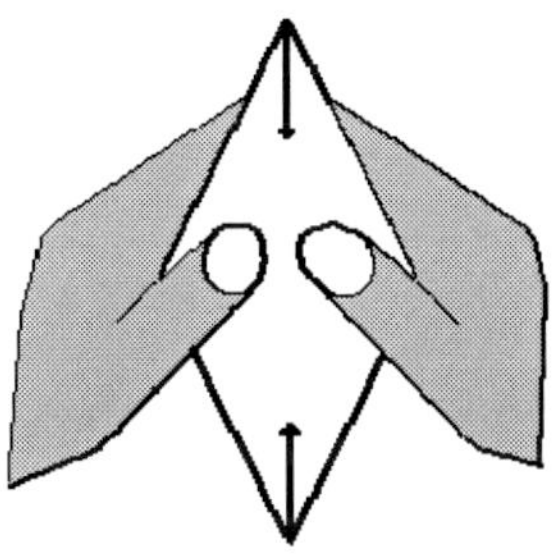

8. With the thumbs inside, lay the upper and lower parts of the hat onto each other.

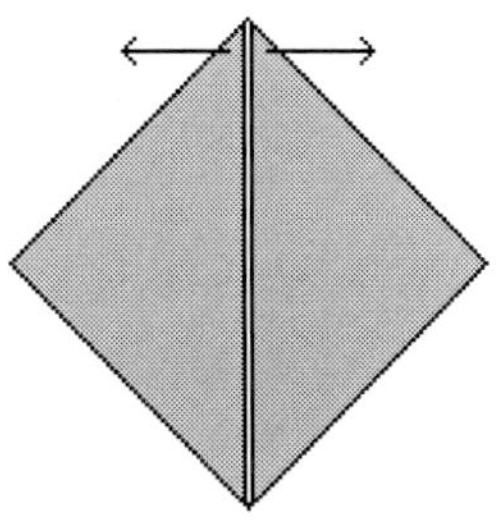

9. Pull the upper corners of the triangles in the directions of the arrows.

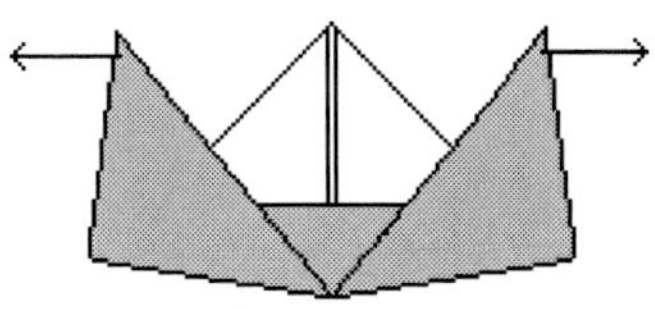

10. Pull the upper corners of the triangles in the directions of the arrows.

YOUR BOAT IS FINISHED

Page 43 'la plage' – the beach

Page 43 :1

Colour the picture

Listen to the CD

Colorie l'image – Colour the picture

This is a listening activity revising words and following colouring instructions.

le ballon ball	la mer sea	le crabe crab	le drapeau flag
le seau bucket	la mouette seagull	le soleil sun	la pelle spade

1. Listen to the CD and colour the pictures accordingly.

CD Script

Colorie le ballon en violet.	Colour the ball purple.
Colorie la mer en bleu.	Colour the sea blue.
Colorie le crabe en rose.	Colour the crab pink.
Colorie le drapeau en jaune.	Colour the flag yellow.
Colorie le seau en vert.	Colour the bucket green.
Colorie la mouette en gris.	Colour the seagull grey.
Colorie le soleil en jaune.	Colour the sun yellow.
Colorie la pelle en rouge.	Colour the spade red.

Page 43 :2

Word search in French

la plage – the beach

This word search can be used for able writers and early learners.

1. The able writers need to copy the words on the dotted lines.
2. The less fluent writers need only find the words in the wordsearch.

For those who like colouring, each relevant letter in the word search can be coloured in. Those who don't like colouring can design patterns in the boxes where the letters are found.

Page 43 :3

Maths in French

Compte, entoure et colorie – Count, circle and colour

1. Revise the words at the top of the page.
2. Revise numbers 1 - 10.
   Ask the children which letter of the alphabet each French number begins with.
   They have difficulty remembering **un**, **quatre** and **cinq**
3. Count the number of pictures, circle that number in French and colour in that same number of dots at the end of the row.

Songs and Ça va?

Songs and Ça va?

This is a good time to revise singing as many songs as you have time for at the end of the lesson.

The circle game/song **Ça va?** and its actions are fully explained on page 45

It is worth learning this little activity song at this stage and revise it often as the spoken French is useful.

Mon nom ....

Colorie l'image

 **violet**

 **bleu**

 **rose**

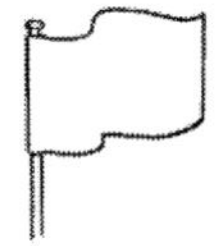 **jaune**

 **vert**

 **gris**

 **jaune**

 **rouge**

Mon nom ....

la plage

b	z	m	e	r	f	n
a	m	z	a	t	o	p
s	o	q	s	y	d	e
o	u	f	v	u	r	l
l	e	k	d	j	u	l
e	t	e	x	v	w	e
i	t	r	s	e	a	u
l	e	v	r	e	b	x

le **seau**

le ....

la **mer**

la ....

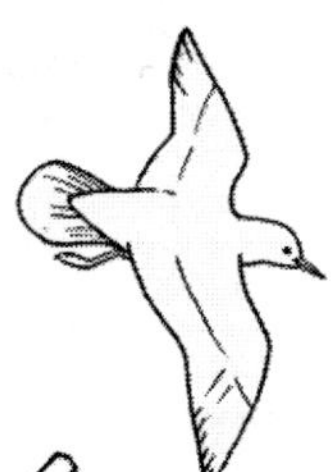

la **mouette**

la ....

le **soleil**

le ....

la **pelle**

la ....

Mon nom ....

Compte, entoure et colorie

 le **seau**  la **mouette**  la **pelle**  la **glace**  le **soleil**

deux
cinq
neuf

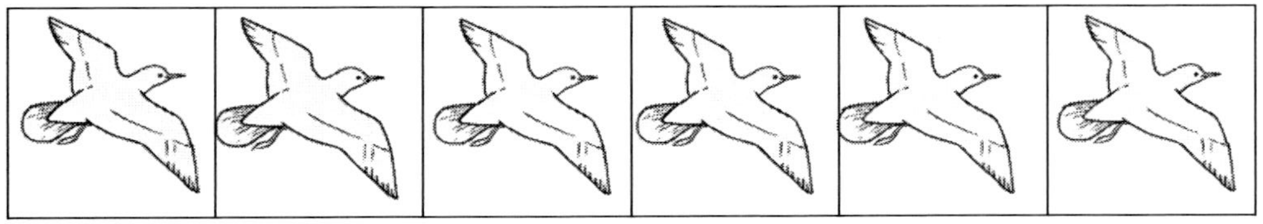

six
trois
cinq

huit
sept
neuf

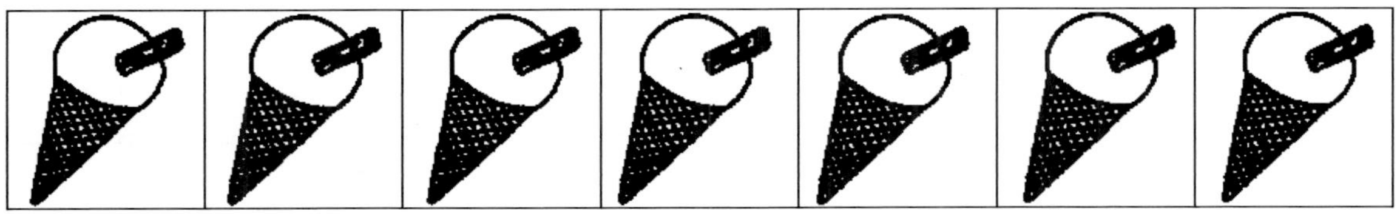

trois
sept
cinq

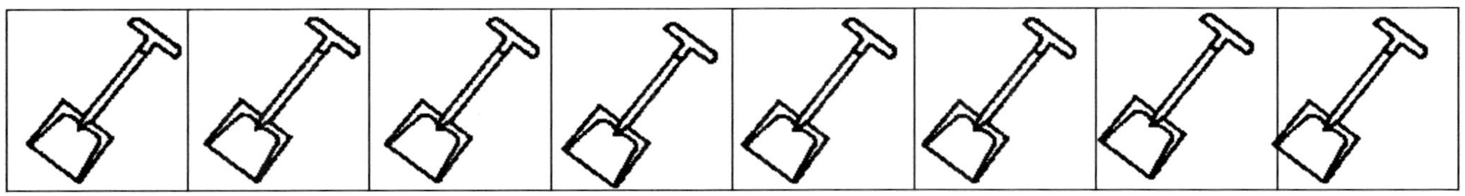

deux
neuf
huit

Page 44 'le transport' – transport

Page 44 :1

Transport loto

listen to the CD

le transport – transport

Go over all the vocabulary with the children and listen to the CD to make sure the children know all the noises the pictures make.

Each child circles one of the four boxes (each box contains six pictures)

Listen to the CD and cross out a picture, in the box you have chosen, when you hear the correct sound.

The winner is the first child to cross out all six pictures.
CD Play track 44 for games 1 & 2
CD Replay track 44 for games 3 & 4

Page 44 :2

Picture association

Forme des paires – make pairs

This exercise is for the children who find writing easy.

All they have to do is write the correct number of the picture associated with each mode of transport and write the name of each mode of transport on the dotted line.

eg The saddle is **1** assocatied with the bike **1**

All worksheets marked **:2** should be neat and accurate.

Page 44 :3

Counting and colouring in French.

Compte et colorie – Count and colour

1. Revise the words at the top of the page.
2. Look at each of the five sentences. 'colorie' means 'colour' in French.
3. All the numbers and colours have symbols beside them to help the early readers.
4. The words in **bold type** show the mode of transport which is shown at the top of the page.
5. This worksheet can be completed by all the children.
6. The more able readers can try and read each sentence.

Pelmanism in French

Pelmanism

Get the children to sit in a circle.
Write the name/draw a picture of one of the ten objects at the top of the loto sheet (44:1) on small pieces of paper (one piece per child) and hand them out to the children.
Choose one child to stand in the middle of the circle.
That child makes the noise of the word/picture on his piece of paper.
He then chooses another child sitting in the circle.
That child makes the noise of the word/picture on his piece of paper.
If they are the same they score a point and sit together as one.
If not, another child is chosen to go in the middle and make his noise.
Keep going until everyone has been chosen or the children get restless.

Mon nom ....

loto

la voiture | le vélo | l'avion | le train | le bus | le loup | la mouette | la mer | le cochon | le chien

Mon nom ....

Forme des paires

la **Voiture**

le **Vélo**

l'**avion**

le **train**

le **bus**

1

....

2

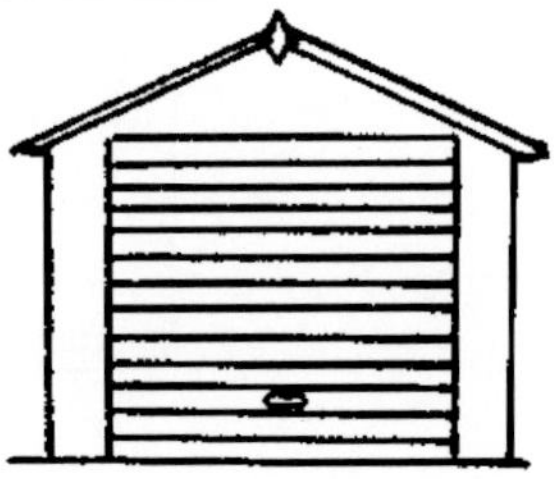

....

3

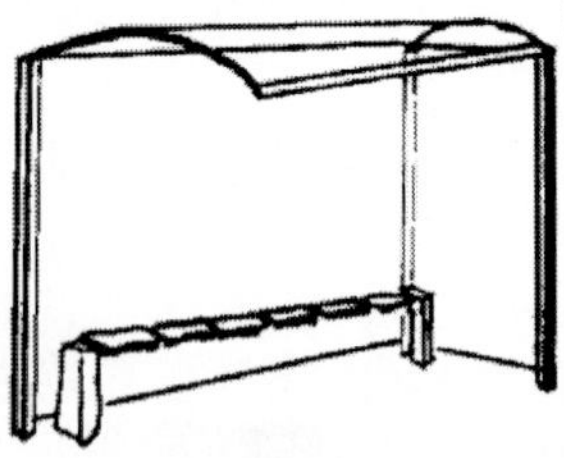

....

4

....

5

....

Mon nom ....

Compte et colorie

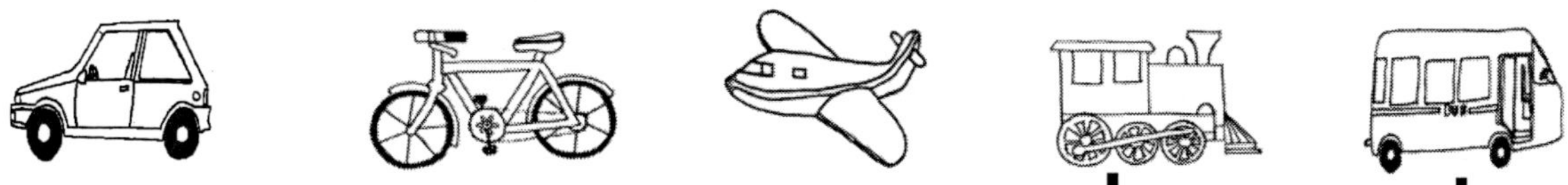

la **Voiture** le **Vélo** l'**avion** le **train** le **bus**

1. Colorie deux 2 **voitures** en jaune. 
2. Colorie cinq 5 **bus** en vert. 
3. Colorie un 1 **train** en bleu. 
4. Colorie quatre 4 **vélos** en rouge. 
5. Colorie trois 3 **avions** en orange. 

Page 45 'Bonjour, ça va?' – Hello, how are you?

Page 45 :1

How are you?

Listen to the CD

Bonjour ça va? – Hello, how are you?

Ask a few children how they are – they should reply "Ça va bien, merci."
Listen to the CD and look at the picture.

CD Script

Bonjour, Hubert! Ça va? **Ça va bien, merci.**
Bonjour, Sophie! Ça va? **Ça va bien, merci.**
Bonjour, Patrice! Ça va? **Ça ne va pas bien.**
Bonjour, Emilie! Ça va? **Comme ci comme ça.**
Bonjour, Gilbert! Ça va? **Comme ci comme ça.**

CD Script of the dance

Children stand in a circle and one goes in the middle. Everyone sings:

Bonjour! Ça va? Bonjour! Ça va?
The children in the circle walk round chanting these questions.

Ça va bien. Ça va bien.
The children in the circle stop and the child in the middle answers.

Bonjour! Ça va? Bonjour! Ça va?
The children in the circle start walking round chanting these questions.

Ça va bien merci.
The children in the circle stop and the child in the middle answers.

Bonjour! Ça va? Bonjour! Ça va?
Ça ne va pas bien. Ça ne va pas bien.
Bonjour! Ça va? Bonjour! Ça va?
Ça ne va pas bien.

Bonjour! Ça va? Bonjour! Ça va?
Comme ci comme ça Comme ci comme ça
Bonjour! Ça va? Bonjour! Ça va?
Comme ci comme ça

Page 45 :2

How are you?

Bonjour ça va?

Look at the six different children, their names and the symbols.

Ask the question "**Ça va?**"
Write the correct answer on the dotted line next to each child's picture. The symbols and answers are at the top of the page.

Revise the questions and answers covered so far in the book.
Page 16 Comment tu t'appelles? Page 26 Quel âge as-tu?
Page 36 Où habites-tu?

Page 45 :3

Spot the difference

Trouve les 10 différences – Spot the difference

1. The bird
2. The giraffe's hoof
3. The giraffe's spots
4. The thistle
5. The mouse's belt
6. The octopus' cap
7. The octopus' foot
8. The elephant's nails
9. The butterfly
10. The mushroom

Mon nom ....

Bonjour, ça va? Bonjour, ça va?

Ça va bien, merci.
I'm fine, thanks.

Ça ne va pas bien.
I don't feel very well.

Comme ci comme ça
So so

Mon nom ....

Bonjour ! Ça va?

Write the correct reply to the questions.

Ça va bien.	Comme ci comme ça.	Ça ne va pas bien.

Lucas	Jade	Enzo

Emma	**Camille**	**Clément**

 **Bonjour, Lucas, ça va?** ....

 **Bonjour, Jade, ça va?** ....

 **Bonjour, Enzo, ça va?** ....

 **Bonjour, Emma, ça va?** ....

 **Bonjour, Camille, ça va?** ....

 **Bonjour, Clément, ça va?** ....

Mon nom ....

Trouve les 10 différences

un kilomètre en vélo

un kilomètre en vélo
deux kilomètres en vélo
allons y allons y
deux kilomètres en vélo

un kilomètre en voiture
deux kilomètres en voiture
allons y allons y
deux kilomètres en voiture

un kilomètre en train
deux kilomètres en train
allons y allons y
deux kilomètres en train

un kilomètre en avion
deux kilomètres en avion
allons y allons y
deux kilomètres en avion

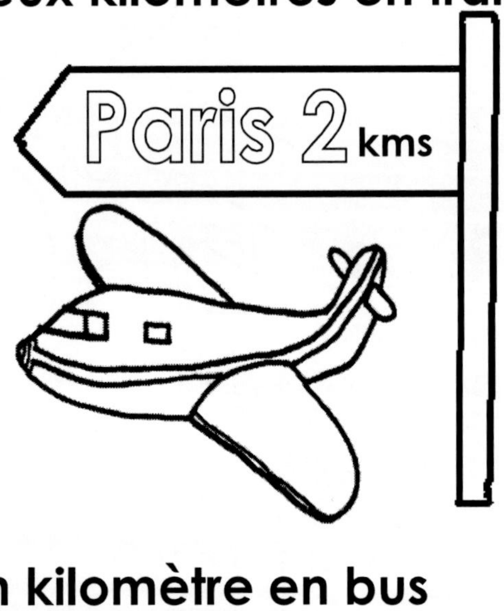

un kilomètre en bus
deux kilomètres en bus
allons y allons y
deux kilomètres en bus

un dé

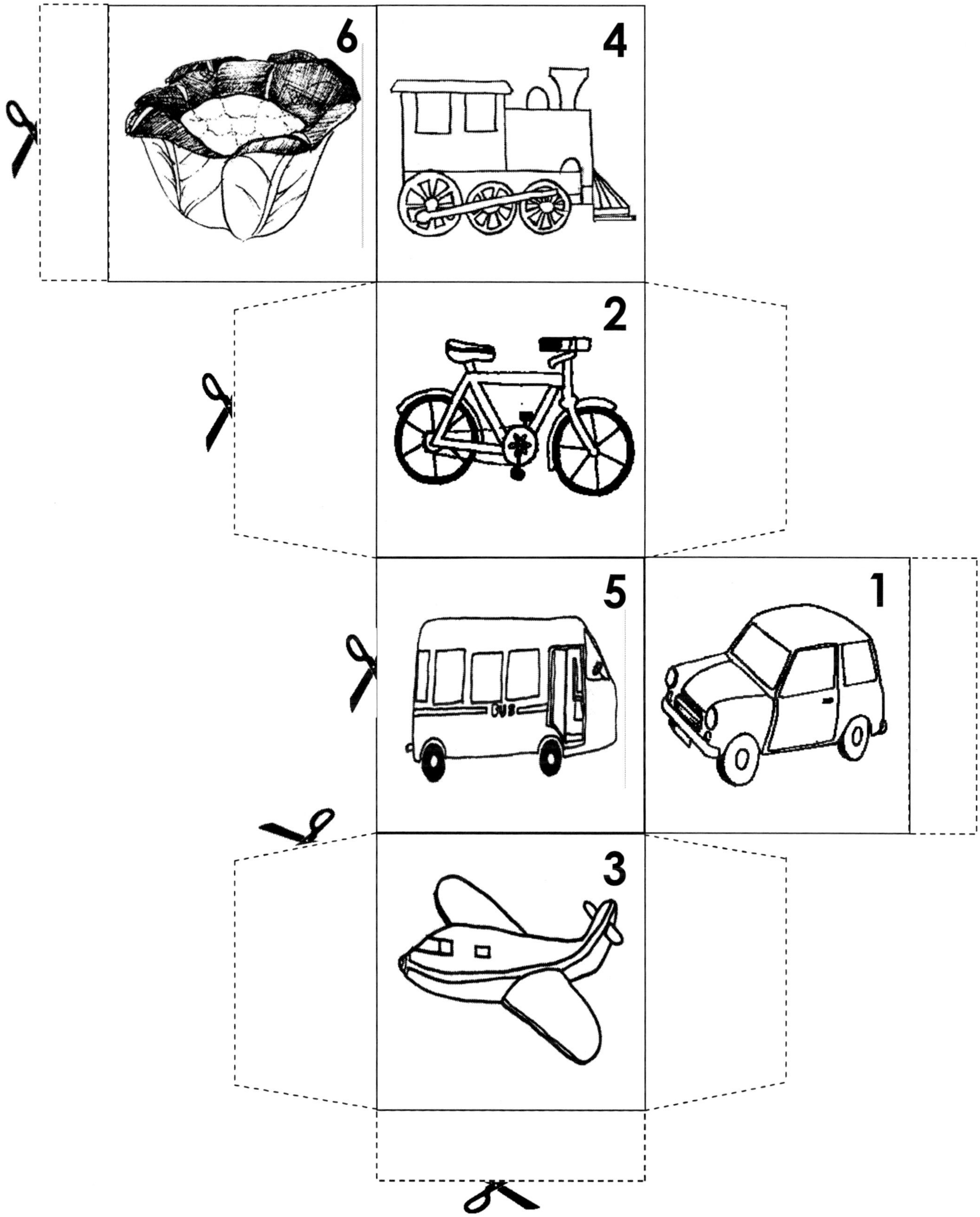

Page 47 'les révisions' – revision

Page 47 :1

Listen & colour

Listen to the CD

Écoute et colorie – Listen and colour

This is a whole class activity and listening exercise.

Go over all the vocabulary before listening to the CD.

Write the correct number in the correct box.

1. La fleur est numéro quatre.
2. La voiture est numéro neuf.
3. Le soleil est numéro six.
4. L'avion est numéro dix.
5. Le renard est numéro trois.
6. La souris est numéro sept.
7. Le papillon est numéro deux.
8. Le vélo est numéro huit.
9. L'arbre est numéro un.
10. Le seau est numéro cinq.

Page 47 :2

Observe and listen in French

loto – bingo

NB When photocopying make sure the teacher has a copy so he/she can tick off the pictures as a reference.

This is a revision exercise for colours, transport and the countryside. All the vocabulary is in picture form (no reading is required).

1st game: Ask the children to colour in 5 colours.
Start reading out the colours.
The children cross out the colours they have coloured in.

The winner is the first child to cross out all 5 pictures.

This game can be played four times (2 x colours 2 x vocabulary).

Page 47 :3

Observe & colour in French

Colorie les images – Colour the pictures

This is an activity for everyone.

It is also a revision exercise for transport.

Before starting the worksheet, try and find all the modes of transport and name them in French.

1. Look at the two halves of each mode of transport.
2. Find the small sample of each mode of transport at the bottom of the page and colour the two halves in their correct colour.

Game

As-tu le bleu?

As-tu le bleu? Have you got the blue? Children sit in a circle

Take ten coloured felt squares and whilst singing '**Frère Jacques**' get the children to pass the felts round in a circle.

On the last word of the song (dong) the children with the felt squares sit on them (the others pretend to do the same).

Children take it in turns to ask each other "As-tu le (whatever colour)?" until the correct child has been asked.

Keep going until all the colours have been discovered.

Singing

If time, choose a song to sing.

Mon nom ....

Écoute et colorie

1	2	3	4	5
l' arbre	le papillon	le renard	la fleur	le seau
6	**7**	**8**	**9**	**10**
le soleil	la souris	le vélo	la voiture	l' avion

Mon nom ....

loto

jaune | bleu | vert | marron | blanc | rouge | orange | violet | noir | rose

la fleur | le seau | la pelle | l' avion | le renard | la souris | le papillon | le vélo | l' arbre | la voiture

jaune | bleu | vert | marron | blanc | rouge | orange | violet | noir | rose

la fleur | le seau | la pelle | l' avion | le renard | la souris | le papillon | le vélo | l' arbre | la voiture

Mon nom ....

Colorie les images

Find and colour the two parts of each mode of transport.
The colour clues are at the bottom of the page.

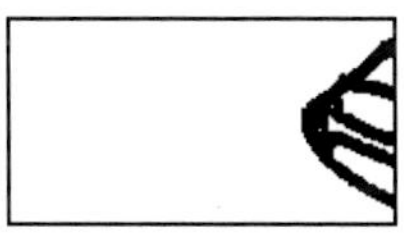 **rouge**

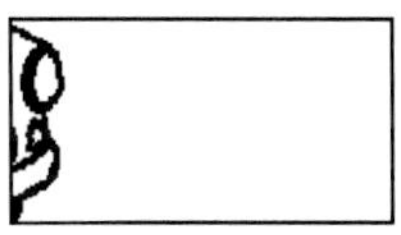 **jaune**

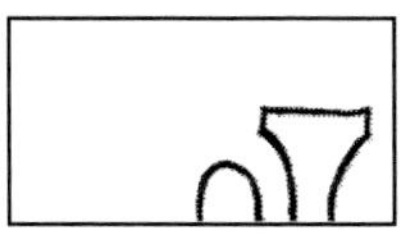 **bleu**

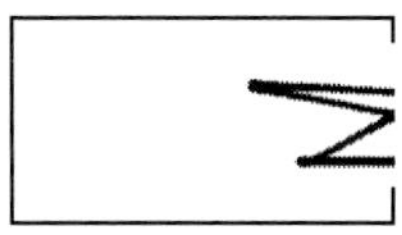 **rose**

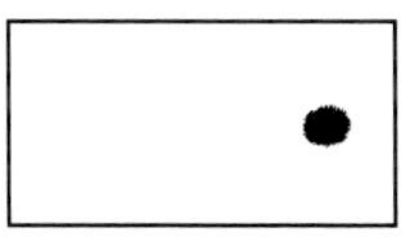 **marron**

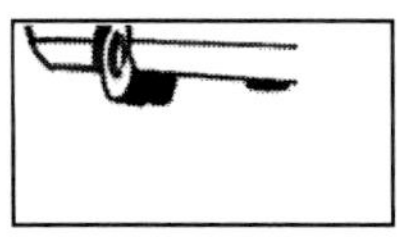 **orange**

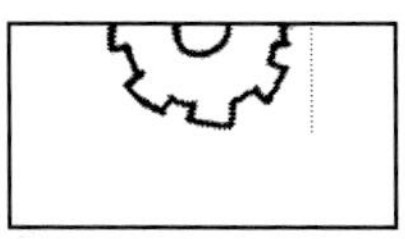 **violet**

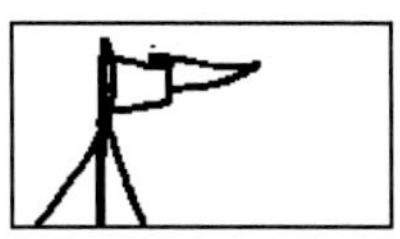 **vert**

Page 48 'chez moi' – at home

Page 48 :1

loto

Listen to the CD

le transport – transport

1. Go over all the vocabulary with the children and listen to the CD to make sure the children know the noises all the pictures make.
2. Each child circles one of the four boxes (each box contains six pictures)
3. Listen to the CD and cross out a picture, in the box you have chosen, when you hear the correct sound.

   The winner is the first child to cross out all six pictures.
   CD Play track 44 for games 1 & 2
   CD Replay track 44 for games 3 & 4

Page 48 :2

How many are there?

Combien de ....y a-t-il? – How many ... are there?

This exercise is for the children who find writing easy.

All they have to do is count the correct number of the objects in the larger picture.
All the numbers are written at the top of the page so accuracy should be no problem. For those who enjoy writing, they can copy the whole sentences on the dotted lines.

All worksheets marked **:2** should be neat and accurate.

Page 48 :3

Spot the difference

Trouve les 10 différences – Spot the difference

1. teddy on the shelf
2. heart on the bed headboard
3. buttons on shirt
4. slat on back of chair
5. shoe under chair
6. television screen
7. knob on drawer
8. book under carpet
9. ear on teddy
10. fringe on carpet

Bonjour ça va?

Song and actions

CD track 45

Bonjour ça va? Children sit in a circle

Bonjour! Ça va? Bonjour! Ça va?
The children in the circle walk round chanting these questions.
Ça va bien. Ça va bien.
The children in the circle stop and the child in the middle answers.
Bonjour! Ça va? Bonjour! Ça va?
The children in the circle start walking round chanting these questions.
Ça va bien merci.
The children in the circle stop and the child in the middle answers.

Bonjour! Ça va? Bonjour! Ça va?
Ça ne va pas bien. Ça ne va pas bien.
Bonjour! Ça va? Bonjour! Ça va?
Ça ne va pas bien.

Bonjour! Ça va? Bonjour! Ça va?
Comme ci comme ça Comme ci comme ça
Bonjour! Ça va? Bonjour! Ça va?
Comme ci comme ça

Mon nom ....

loto

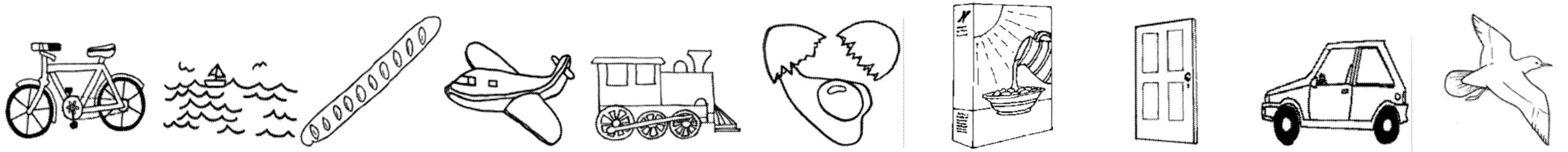

le vélo | la mer | le pain | l'avion | le train | l'oeuf | les céréales | la porte | la voiture | la mouette

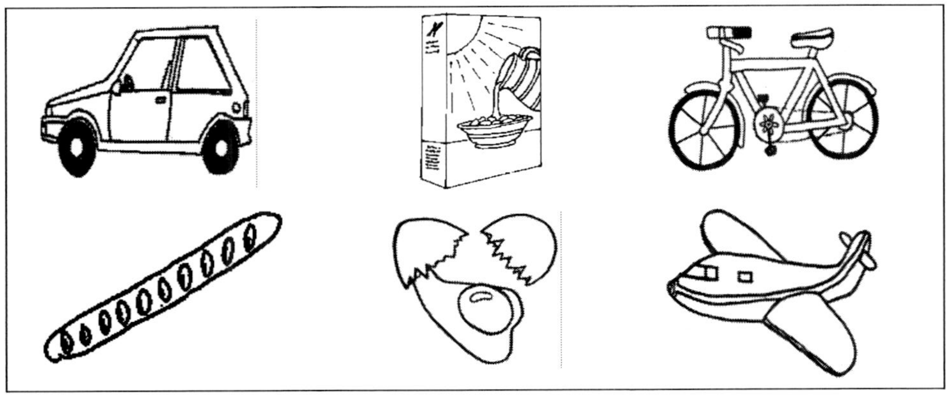

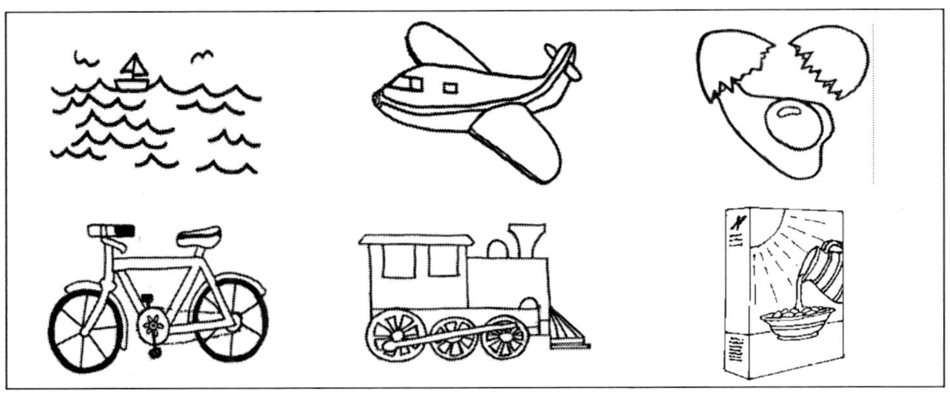

Mon nom ....

Combien de…y a-t-il?

un	deux	trois	quatre	cinq	six	sept	huit	neuf	dix
1	2	3	4	5	6	7	8	9	10

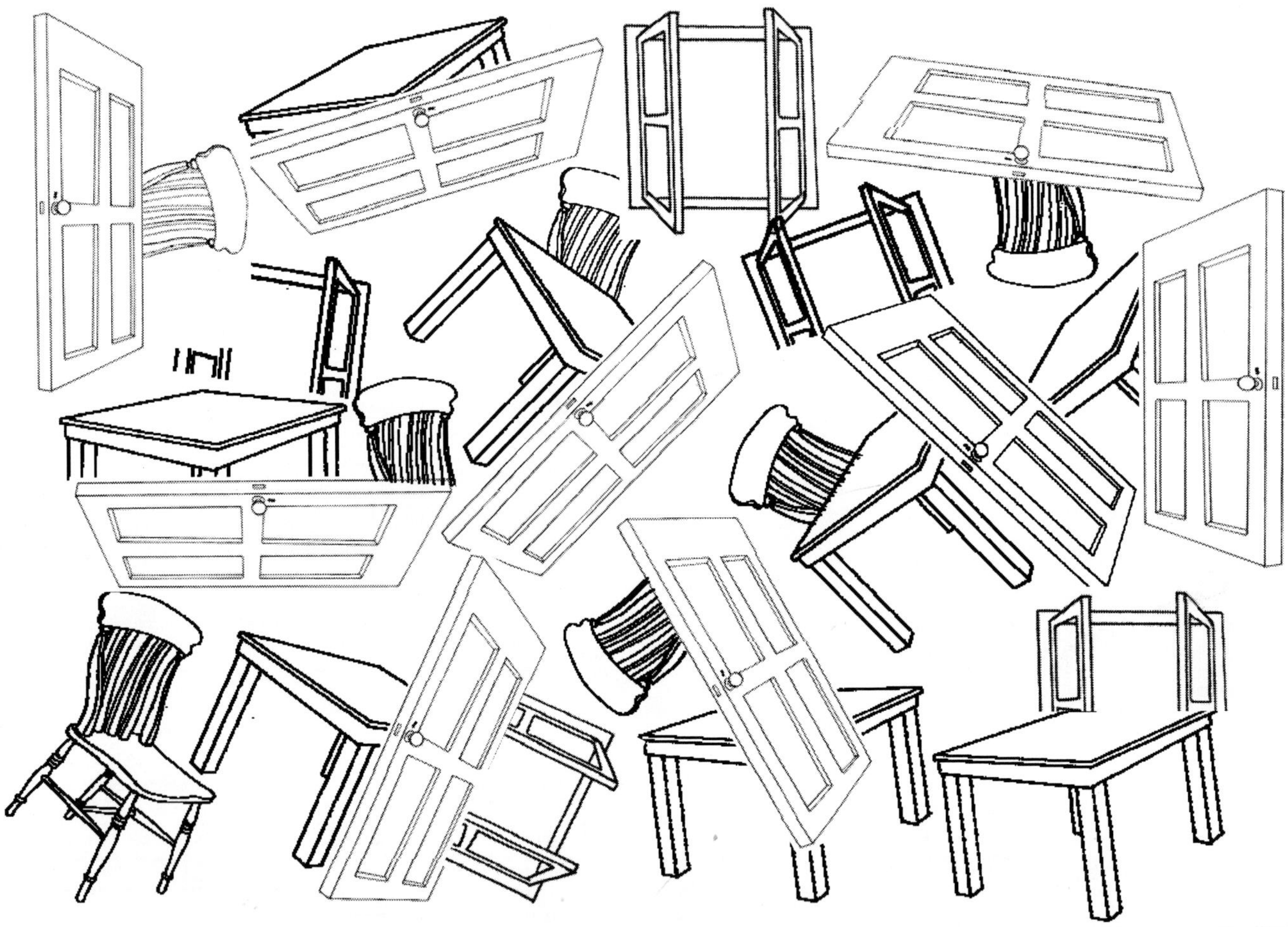

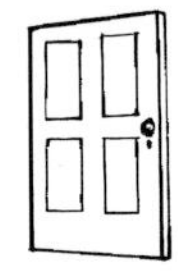

Il y a _ _ _ _ portes.

....

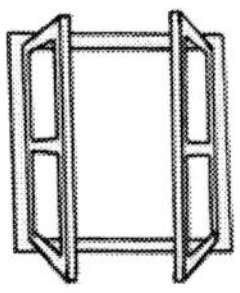

Il y a _ _ _ _ fenêtres.

....

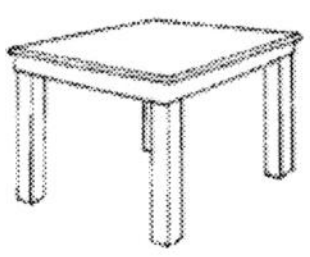

Il y a _ _ _ _ tables.

....

Il y a _ _ _ _ chaises.

....

Mon nom ....

Trouve les dix différences

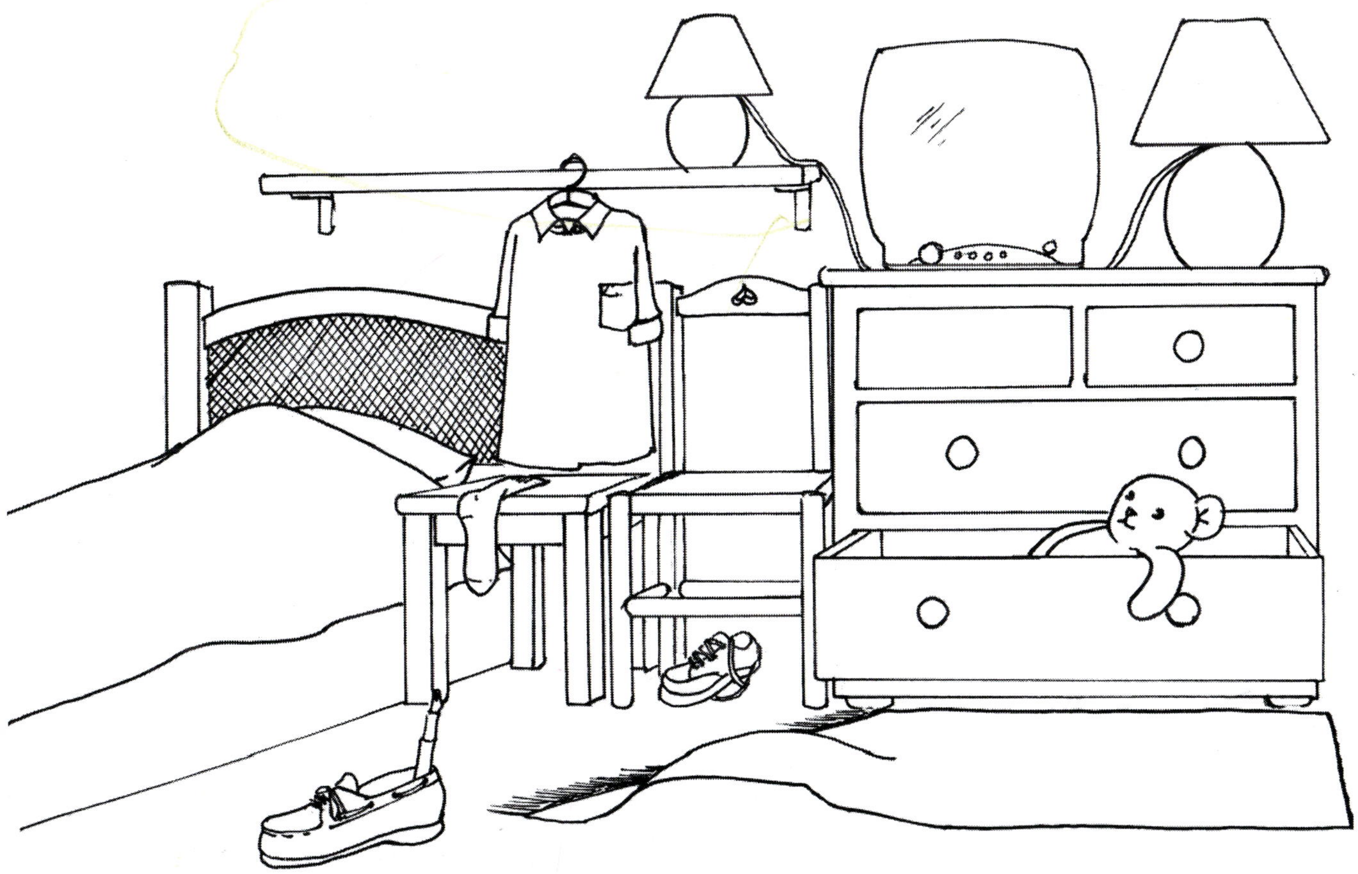

Page 49 'la famille' – the family

Page 49 :1

The family

Listen to the CD

la famille – the family

1. Go over all the vocabulary with the children.
2. Listen to the CD and circle the correct word to complete the sentence.

   Ask some children to read or memorize the sentences.

   Mime one of the eating actions and ask a child to say:
   Tu manges .... You are eating .....

CD Script

Papa mange une pomme.	Daddy is eating an apple.
Maman mange une banane.	Mummy is eating a banana.
David mange un bonbon.	David is eating a sweet.
Anne mange une glace.	Anne is eating an ice-cream.

Page 49 :2

Maths in French

Compte, calcule et écris – Count, add and write.

This exercise is ideal for children who find writing and maths easy.

All they have to do is look up the number which goes with each picture, add the numbers together and write the new number in the answer section, drawing its picture in the box.

All worksheets marked **:2** should be completed neatly and accurately.

Page 49 :3

Observe and write

Écris le bon numbéro dans les formes

Write the correct number in the shapes

Papa **12**	David **11**	la banane **4**	le chien **15**	le chat **9**
Maman **13**	Anne **14**	le bonbon **8**	la glace **5**	la pomme **2**
la souris **10**	le ballon **6**	la porte **3**	la chaise **7**	le placard **1**

The vegetable chant + song
(pg 30)

The vegetable chant + actions

(See pictures on 25:3 for illustrated pictures)

1. Chant **une car otte** and on each syllable tap the head (x 3)
2. Chant **une tom ate** and on each syllable click fingers (x 3)
3. Chant **un oig non** and on each syllable clap hands (x 3)
4. Chant **une pomme d' terre** and on each syllable pat the desk with palms of hands (x 3) (**de terre** can be said as one syllable)
5. As you chant **et un chou-fleur** make a large round circular shape in the air with both hands.

Mon nom ....

ma famille

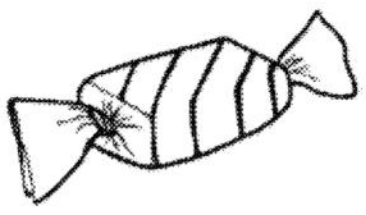	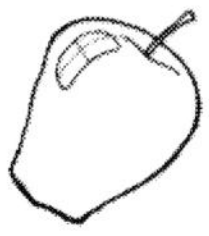		
un **bonbon**	une **pomme**	une **banane**	une **glace**

Papa	**mange**	un **bonbon**	une **pomme**	une **banane**	une **glace**
Maman	**mange**	un **bonbon**	une **pomme**	une **banane**	une **glace**
David	**mange**	un **bonbon**	une **pomme**	une **banane**	une **glace**
Anne	**mange**	un **bonbon**	une **pomme**	une **banane**	une **glace**

Mon nom ....

Compte, calcule et écris

un	deux	trois	quatre	cinq	six	sept	huit	neuf	dix

_ _ _ _ + _ _ _ _ = _ _ _ _

_ _ _ + _ _ _ _ _ = _ _ _ _

_ _ + _ _ _ _ _ _ = _ _ _ _

_ _ _ _ + _ _ _ _ = _ _ _

_ _ _ _ + _ _ = _ _ _ _

Mon nom ....

Écris le bon numéro dans les formes

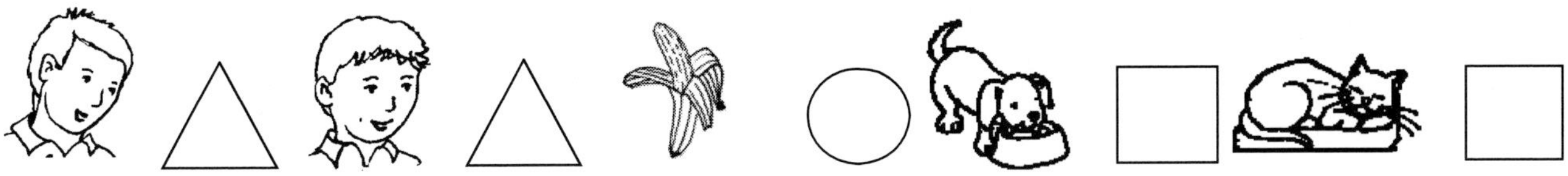

Papa **David** la **banane** le **chien** le **chat**

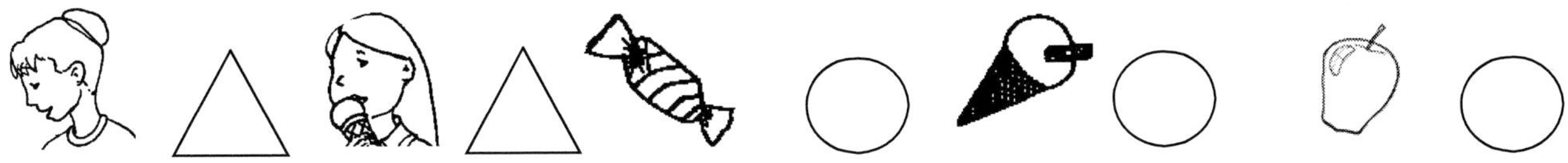

Maman **Anne** le **bonbon** la **glace** la **pomme**

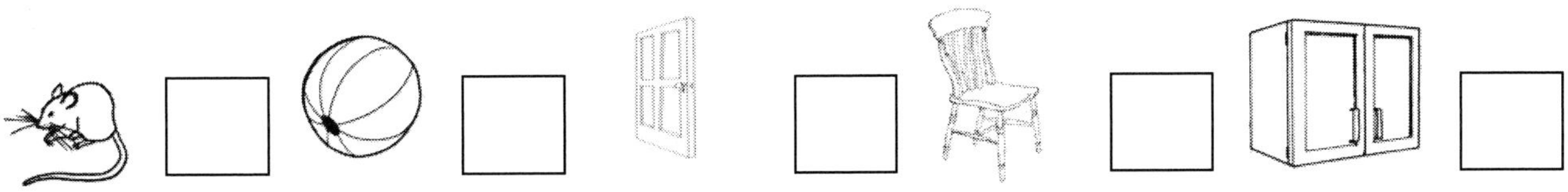

la **souris** le **ballon** la **porte** la **chaise** le **placard**

Papa, Maman, David, Anne

Papa, Maman, David, Anne et le chien 'Coccinelle'
Papa, Maman, David, Anne et le chien 'Coccinelle'
Papa est le père, Maman est la mère
David est le frère
Anne est la soeur
Papa, Maman, David, Anne
et le chien 'Coccinelle'
Papa, Maman, David, Anne
et le chien 'Coccinelle'

this circle on top and visible

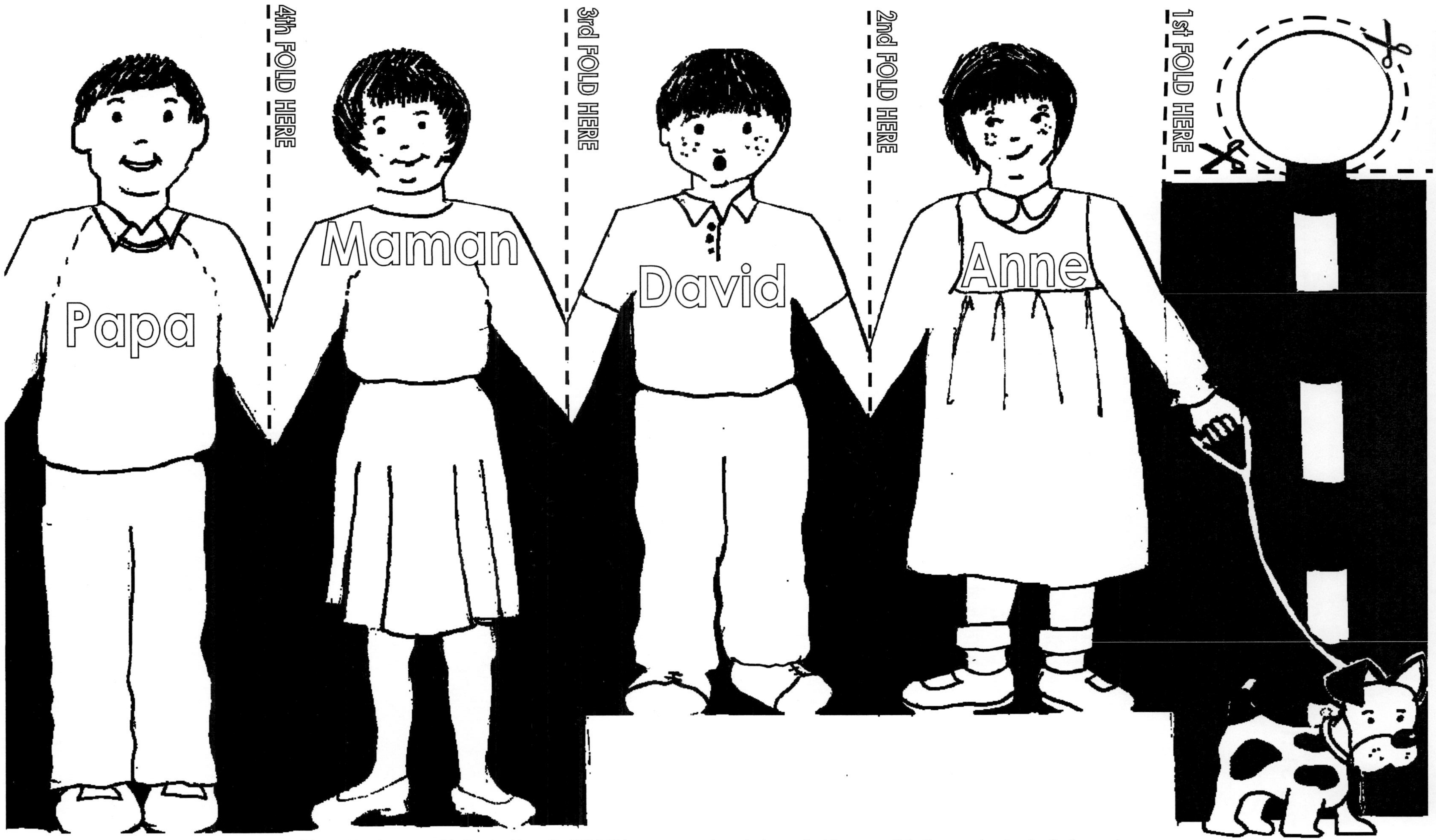

Page 51 'J'ai soif.' – I'm thirsty.

Page 51 :1

Listen and colour the picture

Listen to the CD

Écoute et colorie l'image. – Listen to and colour the picture.

1. Go over all the vocabulary with the children.
2. Listen to the CD and colour the objects in the picture the correct colour.

   Ask the children the colour of each item starting with:
   De quelle couleur est ....? What colour is....?

CD Script

Le ballon est rouge.	The ball is red.
Le lit est bleu.	The bed is blue.
La commode est marron.	The chest of drawers is brown.
Le tapis est violet.	The carpet is purple.
Le nounours est orange.	The teddy is orange.
La lampe est jaune.	The lamp is yellow.

Page 51 :2

Science in French

Mélange les couleurs – Mix the colours

This exercise is aimed at helping children know which primary colours join to make new colours.

Make sure the children know which two primary colours make **GREEN**, **PURPLE** and **ORANGE.**
The children can design and colour the droplets as they wish.

All worksheets marked **:2** should be completed neatly and accurately.

Page 51 :3

Maths in French

Compte et calcule Count and work out

Look at the drinks at the top of the page and their equivalent numbers.

Find the same picture on the left hand side of the page and colour in any two numbers in the row that add up to the value of each picture.
eg **GLASS** (5) **1 2 3 4 5 6**

If there is more than one combination making up the final number each combination can be coloured differently.

Choosing time for all the songs

Choosing time for all the songs.

The children have learned many traditional and Skoldo songs in this book.

Use the end of the lesson to choose and sing any favourite song.

Ask the children why they have chosen a certain song.

Mon nom ....

Écoute et colorie l'image

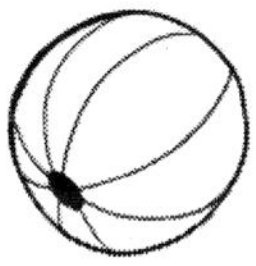

Le ballon est rouge.

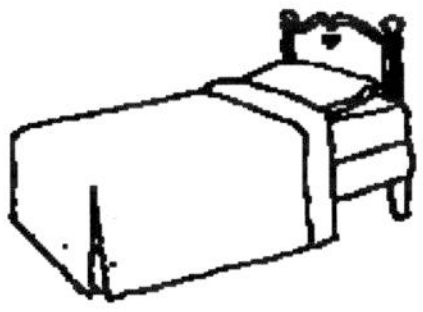

Le lit est bleu.

La commode est marron.

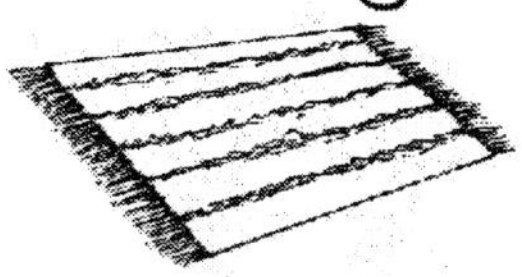

Le tapis est violet.

Le nounours est orange.

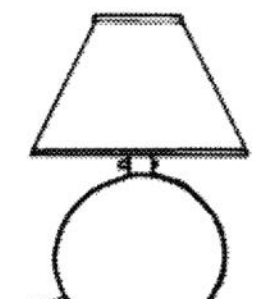

La lampe est jaune.

Mon nom ....

Mélange les couleurs

bleu **rouge** **jaune** **violet** **orange** **vert**

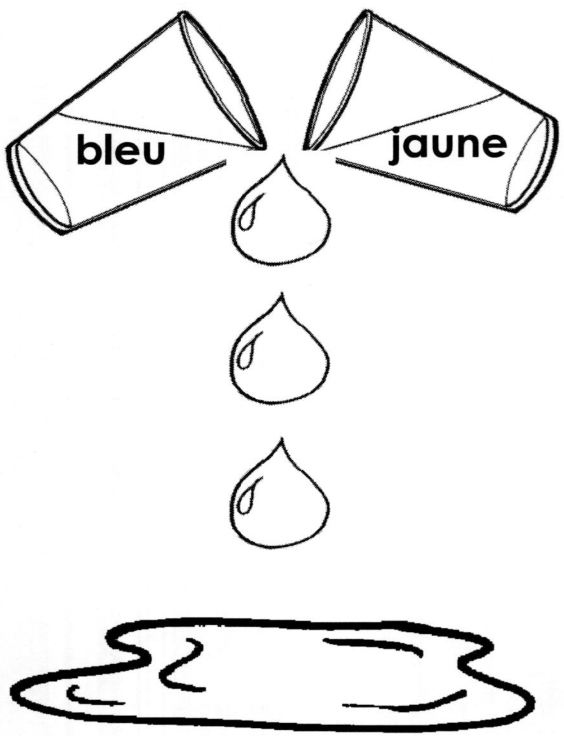

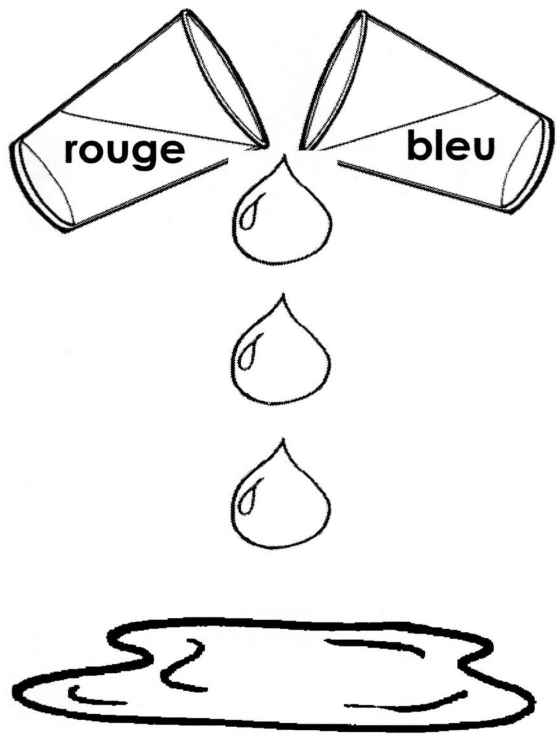

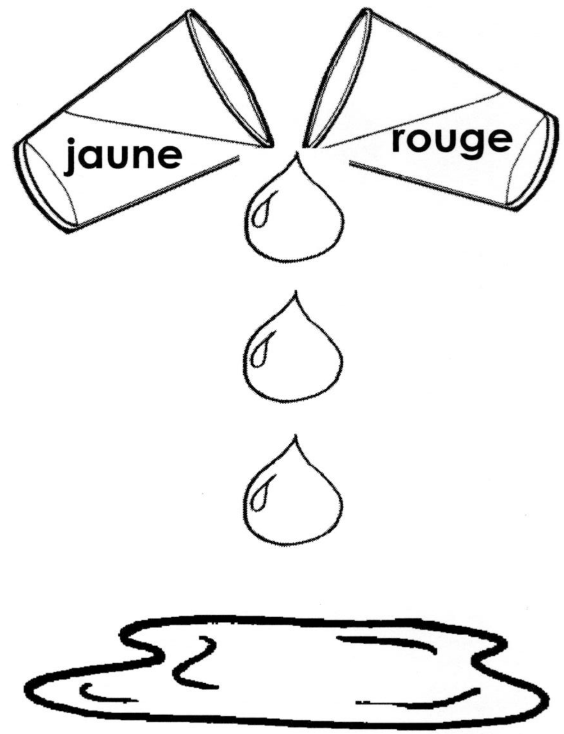

___ ___ ___ ___ ___ ___ ___ ___ ___ ___ ___ ___ ___ ___ ___ ___

Mon nom ....

Compte et calcule

Colour any two numbers which add up to make the picture's number.

3 trois **5 cinq** **7 sept** **9 neuf** **10 dix**

	1	2	3	4	5	6
	1	2	3	4	5	6
	1	2	3	4	5	6
	1	2	3	4	5	6
	1	2	3	4	5	6

Page 52 'la trousse' – the pencil case

Page 52 :1

Circle the pictures

Listen to the CD

Entoure les images. – Circle the pictures.

1. Go over all the vocabulary with the children.
2. Listen to the CD and circle in the main picture each object as it is mentioned.

CD Script

Entoure le livre.	Circle the book.
Entoure le poisson.	Circle the fish.
Entoure le pinceau.	Circle the paintbrush.
Entoure le taille-crayon.	Circle the pencil sharpener.
Entoure la gomme.	Circle the rubber.
Entoure le stylo.	Circle the pen.
Entoure la règle.	Circle the ruler.
Entoure le crayon.	Circle the pencil.

Page 52 :2

Find the letters in French words

Cherche et colorie les lettres – Look for and colour the letters

This exercise is aimed at helping children recognize letters and spelling.

Each picture is labelled in French.
Find circle or colour all the letters that make up the French word for each picture.

All worksheets marked **:2** should be completed neatly and accurately.

Page 52 :3

Beware of the cauliflowers

Attention aux choux-fleurs! – Beware of the cauliflowers!

This is a dice game which can be played twice.
Fold the page in two (along the dotted line) so you can only see one game at a time.

The teacher throws a dice and reads out the number followed by the French for the picture in the box.

The aim of the game is to colour in (very quickly) all the pictures before three 6s (the cauliflowers) have been thrown.

If you can get each child to throw the dice and play the game this way, it is more exciting but less controllable!

Choosing time for songs and games

Choosing time for songs and games

The children have learned many songs and games in this book.
Use the end of the lesson to choose any song or game they wish.

Find out the reasons behind their choices.

Mon nom ....

Entoure les images.

le **livre**

le **poisson**

le **pinceau**

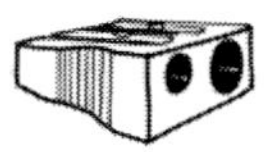
le **taille-crayon**

la **gomme**

le **stylo**

la **règle**

le **crayon**

Mon nom ....

Cherche et colorie les lettres

la **gomme**

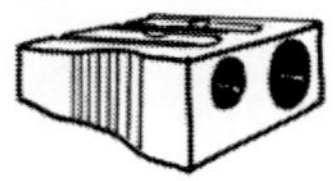
le **taille-crayon**

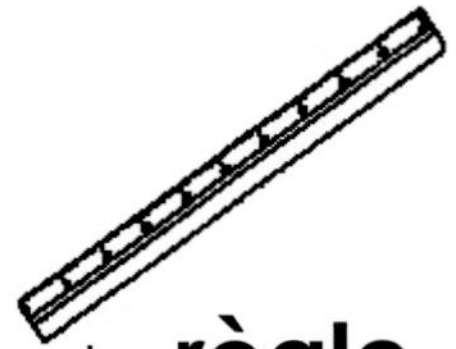
la **règle**

le **crayon**

le **stylo**

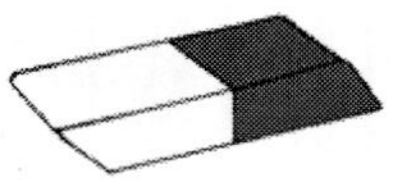 b v g d o l n s m j p n m e i

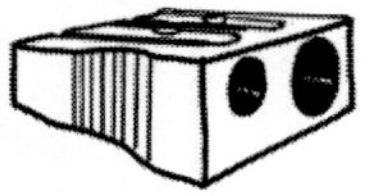 p t v a i l m l e c r j a y s o n

 z j c r p è g o l d i k e w u t b

 g c m f r k a q y i z o s n x e

 c m s q v t u s r y w l n o x

✍ Mon nom ....

Attention aux choux-fleurs!

Bonne nuit, dors bien

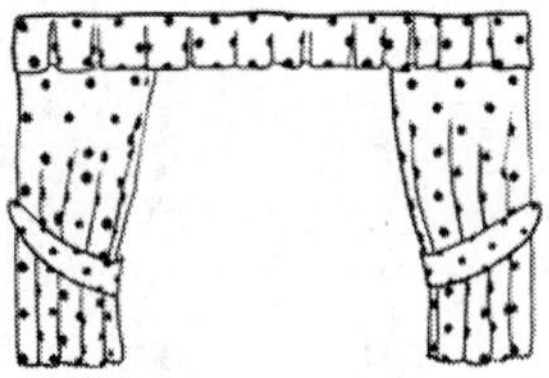

Bonne nuit, dors bien
Chut! Ferme les rideaux
Bonne nuit, dors bien
Chut! Ferme les yeux

les étoiles, la lune
la chauve-souris
le hibou, le blaireau
et le renard

Bonne nuit, dors bien
Chut! Ferme les rideaux
Bonne nuit, dors bien
Chut! Ferme les yeux

Mon nom ....